CREEK WITH NO NAME

How the West Was Won (and Lost)
in Gaston, Oregon

By Ken Bilderback

First runner-up, History Prize
2012 New York Book Festival

Honorable Mention,
2012 San Francisco Book Festival
and 2012 Hollywood Book Festival

Assisted by Kris Bilderback

www.kenbilderback.com

To Marvin Runyon

Hope you enjoy it!

[signature]

1-16-2013

About the cover

Look at the photo on the cover. Notice the remnants of crops in the semi-drained bed of Wapato Lake? The picture hasn't changed much in the past 100 years or so.

Now imagine yourself standing in the spot where this photo was taken, gazing across the lakebed at Gaston, there on the hill, less than a mile away.

Close your eyes and imagine the sounds: the whistle of a steam locomotive, the clanking of valves on a handful of Model Ts, the distant clatter and whinnying of horses, hitched to their wagons while their owners shop in the market ... That was Gaston 100 years ago.

Now open your eyes and look a little closer at the photo on the cover. It was taken on May 11, 2011.

So please enjoy the book and remember: Any pre-conceived image you have of Gaston might be just an illusion ...

Oh, and just to be clear, the photo of us on Page 277 wasn't taken 100 years ago, either.

Table of Contents

Me and Joe Gaston

Joseph Gaston was a newspaper man. So was I. Joseph Gaston was a disillusioned man. So was I.

Oh, and the similarities don't end there. Joseph Gaston came to Oregon from Ohio, as did I. Joseph Gaston fell in love with Oregon as a young man, as did I. Later in life, Joseph Gaston was attracted to an odd little area where the Tualatin River runs wild past Wapato Lake, as was I, although by the time I got here the river wasn't wild and the lake wasn't a lake.

Oh, and like me, Joseph Gaston became, late in life, an amateur historian.

Joseph Gaston was, in fact, one of Oregon's greatest historians, writing the first definitive volume of the state's founding. He wrote about almost every aspect and community of Oregon, with one glaring exception: Joseph Gaston didn't write about the town that bears his name. There's more than a little irony in that fact, because the history of the little town of Gaston is an almost perfect metaphor for how the West was won by a few ... and lost by almost everyone else. Even more than that, Gaston serves as a perfect model for the arrogance and foibles of Manifest Destiny's true believers, and for the often tenuous grip the rest of us have on what still can be, at times, a very wild Wild West.

That's where I come in. In my own amateur way, I'll try to tell of the events that transpired in and around what is now Gaston. I'll try to tell some of the stories that Old Joe

Gaston could have told, had he chosen to, in his four-volume opus, *The Centennial History of Oregon*. When the books were published in 1912, they could have contained the story of how Gaston was an epicenter for mistreatment of Native Americans and how Gaston is a prime example of how after the Federal government took the land from the Indians it turned right around and gave most it away again, some to people who used the free land they were given to become very greedy tycoons, wholly unappreciative of the gifts they had been given by American taxpayers.

Fortunately, those greedy tycoons were just a sliver of the people who settled the area around Gaston, which is, in many respects, the dead end of the Oregon Trail. Most of the hardy settlers who got Donation Land Claims around these parts were settling for the crumbs left behind after the earliest pioneers gobbled up the prime farmlands of the Willamette Valley. The vast majority of this area's settlers were not at all greedy or famous, but they created another compelling story Joe Gaston could have written, a story of how ordinary people laid a foundation on which later generations have built our own version of the American Dream.

I'll also try to tell some of the stories Joe Gaston couldn't have told, by picking up from the day he died. Joe Gaston wasn't around when, just a few months after his death, August Lovegren's Utopian dreams came crashing down along with the dam he built in Cherry Grove. Gaston would have cheered if he had lived a few years longer to see another of Lovegren's dreams, shared by the Seventh-day Adventists in nearby Laurelwood, become a reality with the passage of Prohibition. Joe Gaston was all for Prohibition, but never foresaw the Prohibition-era moonshiners who hid out in the valleys around his namesake village. He certainly couldn't have known that the antics of the bootleggers would become precursors to an even more dangerous war on drugs 50 years later, all played out, once again, in Gaston.

Joe Gaston didn't live long enough to tell the story of how the area's wealth of natural resources would lead to an epic battle in the class war triggered by the transition from the Agrarian Age to the Industrial Age. Nor did he live to see the hills around Gaston become the bull's eye for the most-concentrated 20th Century wartime attack on continental American soil. Back in Joe Gaston's day forest fires were relatively rare, so it's doubtful he would have predicted that the Tillamook Burn, the granddaddy of all forest fires, would start just a few miles from his old home.

Joe Gaston might have written about some of those developments, but certainly not about the ghost stories or sightings of UFOs and Bigfoot that made the cut for my book. Nor would he have included in his two volumes of biographies stories of most of the people I find fascinating: Staff Jennings, Red Earle, Charles Martin, Hermann Rauschning, Louis Rader, Levi Lovegren, Ferdinand Waldo DeMara, etc. If rumor is to be believed, Gaston charged his biographical subjects to be included in his books; my subjects would have been more likely to pay me to be excluded from mine.

But perhaps the main reason Joe Gaston didn't chronicle the history of the town of Gaston is that his time here was in many ways the nadir of his life, the setting for both his wildest dreams and greatest failures. All of which once again makes Gaston the man and Gaston the town metaphors for the American West.

By the time Gaston wrote *The Centennial History of Oregon* he had been gone from the shores of Wapato Lake for many years and had written another definitive history book, *Portland: Its History and Builders*, about a town he had lived in longer – and seemed to love much more – than the hamlet that bears his name.

Perhaps Gaston the town held bittersweet memories for the man who founded it. Gaston the man came to what would be Gaston the city at something of a low point in his life. After coming to Oregon from Ohio, Gaston settled in Jacksonville and built a law practice, while also resuming his career in newspapers at the *Jacksonville Sentinel*, before becoming editor of the *Salem Statesman*, one of Oregon's largest papers. By the 1860s, however, he had caught the railroad bug and set his sights on cashing in on the invention that was creating the nation's richest men. For 15 years he pursued his dream, rising to become one of the state's premier railroaders, but also playing a pivotal role in what one historian called "The Great Blunder." Offered financing by the British to build what would have been Oregon's greatest railroad, Gaston yielded to the likes of Ben Holladay and J.C. Ainsworth. Eventually a combination of blunders by Ainsworth and deception by Holladay left Gaston deeply in debt and on the outside looking in. Now more a bit player than star in the railroad industry, Gaston had to settle for a lesser dream of a spur line through the Wapato Gap and into the Yamhill Valley.

Joseph Gaston's 15 years in the village that bears his name were a mixed bag, from what little is known of that period in his life. Embroiled in legal and business disputes, he tried to make the most of what opportunities existed in the corridor between Forest Grove and McMinnville, far from the now bustling Willamette Valley corridor of Eugene, Salem and Portland. To that end, his most-ambitious project involved Wapato Lake, a murky body of water that was the very reason Native Americans had been drawn to the area for centuries. But when Gaston looked out over the lake he didn't want to sustain it. He wanted to drain it.

Gaston spoke of his love for nature, but his love was a form of the tough love that was common in the late 1800s: to truly appreciate nature, we had to first conquer and control it. To explain his vision, he used a phrase that also was common in his day: He sought to "reclaim" the land, a phrase that held some special irony during his years of battling with the lake.

Of course he wasn't really "reclaiming" anything. Instead he was claiming title to the lake that the Native Americans considered nearly sacred. The lake was a prize that tribes had fought over, sustaining life by drawing wildlife to its shores and nurturing a root vegetable – the wappatoo, or wapato. Given the lake in a treaty with white settlers, the Indians had it snatched away from them when Congress changed its mind and reneged on the deal. There's no record of whether Joe Gaston recognized the irony in the fact that the Indians lost title to the lake because of the same sort of government dirty dealing that cost him the rights to the Willamette Valley railroad.

After the politicians took back the lake they decided they didn't really want it, and offered it up free to anyone willing to "reclaim" it as farm land. It was easy for Gaston to claim the title for the lake from Congress, but reclaiming the lake from nature would prove much more difficult. Although an anonymous biographer in the foreword to his history of Portland credits Gaston with "reclaiming Wappatoo Lake and converting a disease-breeding swamp into a beautiful farm," the truth of the matter was as murky as the lake itself. First, some might quibble with using the word beautiful to describe the vast onion farm that caused residents to nestle their settlement upwind from the prevailing breezes. More importantly, Mother Nature had her own definition of reclamation, and she tended to prevail in her efforts to reclaim the land for herself. On one hand, the routine flooding of the farmland served Gaston's purposes, revitalizing the land with nutrients for his summer crop. But it also played havoc with his dikes and sloughs, which weren't really perfected until many years after he gave up the effort and moved back to Portland in 1896. There, he pursued other business ventures and his love for history, producing the books that gave him his most-lasting legacy.

I, too, came to Oregon from Ohio, where I worked at *The Dayton Daily News*. For the next 24 years I lived in Portland and passionately pursued a career in newspapering, until a combination of incompetence and treachery among colleagues left me disillusioned and feeling, I suspect, much as Joseph Gaston had when he retreated to the shores of

Wapato Lake 125 years earlier. Casting aside my tarnished lifelong dream, my wife and I found a little plot of land overlooking Wapato Lake in the distance. Our land is downwind from the onion farm, but that no longer matters because about all that remains of that legacy is an alley in town named Onion Lane. When we bought the house we had no idea the farm had ever existed. In fact we didn't know the lake had ever existed.

It wasn't until a few months later that I learned the decrepit buildings along Gaston Road are the remnants of Joseph Gaston's efforts to "reclaim" nature. By now people had pretty much given up on efforts to control the lake for agriculture. When the winter rains came our first year here we saw the ghost of Wapato Lake, as nature reclaimed part of the fallow farmland with the annual flood. Joseph Gaston had viewed these floods as a defeat. I saw them as a victory, both for nature and for the future of the town, which by now was desperately in need of revitalization. A restored lake, I thought, could help make the area the draw it had been for the Indians. But even in this critical difference, it turned out Joseph Gaston and I share a trait: Our views of Wapato Lake reflect the thinking of our times. A few years after we moved here, serious efforts began to restore the lake to its natural state.

In another bit of irony, before I knew the story of Joe Gaston and his lofty effort to reclaim the lake from nature, I had started my own much more modest campaign to reclaim *for* nature a little creek that feeds the lake.

I've come to think I love the Gaston area more than the man who founded and named it. Joseph Gaston became restless in his time here, moving back to the city and re-inventing himself as an industrialist. The longer I'm here, the less restless I become. Never as ambitious as Joseph Gaston, I harbor no desire to return to the city and even less to subject myself to the abuses of corporate interests. Joe Gaston was a corporate industrialist until the day he died, but even here he and I were not so very different in some respects. Until the day he died, Joe Gaston spoke out against the abuses of unregulated commerce and for the right of a democratic society to protect its interests from multinational corporations.

Despite our differences, I flatter myself with comparisons to Joseph Gaston. His anonymous biographer says "Mr. Gaston has always been an independent thinker, forming his opinions from close observation and thorough investigation of the subject that has claimed his attention, and from his studies and experience of life he has devolved a philosophy that has its root in those things which have the definite value in character building and in the real progress of the world."

I suppose that's what any good journalist strives for, so we have that in common. We also know that Joseph Gaston's retreat to rural life overlooking Wapato Lake was a time of some introspection, a time in which he pursued his passion for history and conducted research that led him to a career as an historian. My time of introspection has led me in the same direction, but again with a decided difference. While Gaston looked outward from the town that bears his name to record the history of the rest of the state, I look ever more inward at this one little speck of Oregon's history he seemed to ignore.

It's hard to know if Joseph Gaston was proud of the community he abandoned, but I know I am. The town of Gaston is the direct result of the expansionist dreams of the late 1880s and of the grand visions of the Industrialists, yet ironically it remains a dot on the map that never fell victim to the grandiose and often fatally flawed greed that drove some of those Industrialists. Over the years everyone from timber barons to labor unions have tried to claim the area's people for their own purposes, but the people always manage to reclaim their lives and their stubbornly agrarian culture.

The most recent major developments all suggest that culture is here to stay. The Adventists gave up on their agrarian dream in Laurelwood, but the people who replaced them, the Ananda Church of Self Realization, picked up right where they left off. The onion and dairy farmers gave up, too, but their replacements are organic winegrowers and alpaca ranchers. The federal government is reclaiming Wapato Lake for nature more than 150 years after claiming it from the Indians and giving it away to people who claimed to know how to reclaim it from nature.

Rather than sharing Joe Gaston's dreams of "reclaiming" nature, many of us who live here now are happy to let nature reclaim us.

Me and Joe Gaston. So much alike, and yet so very different ...

Wrestling with Water Monsters

This is sort of a scary story, made much scarier by the fact that "the footprints of this monster can still be seen at Gaston, Oregon."

The monster himself is pretty tame. He's a bully and also a dreamer, but ultimately too clumsy and ineffectual to realize his dreams or to scare away those he tried to intimidate.

But don't stop reading, because this really is a scary story. After reading it some people will be too scared to look in the mirror, not because the monster might be lurking behind them, but rather because they might see just a little bit of the monster in their own image. I warned you. It's a scary story.

"Long ago the people saw it," Kalapuya tribal legend tells us, and what the people saw was horrific. They saw the terrible Water Being of Wapato Lake put two children "on his horn and carry them away to the forked mountain."

Hearing of this tragedy from his only remaining son, the children's father rushed toward the forked mountain and called out frantically for his children, who responded only with cries of "We are different now! Different!" Dejected, the father returned alone, only to find his remaining son dead.

Thus is born Gaston area residents' conflicted love-hate relationship with water.

Wapato Lake drew Native Americans to its banks long before Joseph Gaston came along in the 1860s. The lake made the upper Tualatin Plains a major draw for the Kalapuya tribes.

Joseph Gaston saw visions of wealth in the shimmering lake, and on its shores he built the town that bears his name. Of course in Gaston's eyes, that shimmering water actually hid the true treasure: the fertile land that lay beneath it. He quickly dug a slough to drain it. Starting in the 1870s the town fathers battled to drain the lake, and by the 1890s the men thought they were winning the battle to make Wapato Lake history.

The Kalapuya's Water Being apparently had a similar disdain for the lake, according to the legend passed down for centuries until it was recorded by a group of anthropologists in the 1940s. The Water Being wanted to live in Wapato Lake but found it too confining to swim in. That's when he impaled the children on his horn and carried them off, digging a slough with his tail and draining the lake as he went in search of a bigger place to swim. The desperate father followed the beast's tracks to the other side of the valley toward the forked mountain that the Indians held sacred and which we now call South Saddle Mountain. We don't know what the Indians called the valley, but today we call it Patton Valley. The father tracked the monster to the end of the valley but couldn't find it or his children. All he found was the enormous empty hole that the monster had left behind in its failed attempt to create a lake deep enough to swim in.

The father then followed the Water Being's tracks up and over the ridge into the next valley, the one we call Scoggins Valley, where he heard his children playing. The valley had been turned upside down, legend tells us, with the roots of the trees pointed upward. He called to his children, who responded again with only "We are different! Different!" Dejected, he returned to the shores of the now drained Wapato Lake, where he dreamed about the forked mountain where his children now lived. In his dreams, there was a lake there now, a lake in which he, the Water Being and his children all could swim.

The first white settlers agreed with the Water Being's assessment of Wapato Lake. It never did make much of a swimming hole. It did, however, make a spectacular onion field once it was drained. The fact that the land would nurture root vegetables was no surprise, because the lake was named after the "wapato," a starchy root crop similar to a potato that had sustained the Indians. On the high ground of the growing town of Gaston, the railroad and lumber mills grew. In the low lands, Japanese laborers lived in shacks along Onion Lane, harvesting the crop to load onto the railcars south of town.

But in reality, man never really has tamed the Water Being's old haunt, Wapato Lake. Joseph Gaston tried for a couple of decades after acquiring the lake from the federal government as part of the Swamp Act. While he managed to drain it each year after the rains of winter revitalized the soil, the rain inevitably refilled it every fall. Occasionally the lake could turn into a bit of a monster when the rain became too intense and the lake flooded, cutting off the town from its neighbors, but it always backed off by the oppressive heat of July.

Finally Joseph Gaston gave up on the lake and moved to Portland, leaving the task of taming the lake to others. For the next 40 years men wrestled with the beast until, in 1936, victory was declared with the construction of a massive dike that was certain to last. When the rains came in October, the dike did indeed hold. November kept pouring it on, and the dike held. Even December, typically the rainiest month, proved no match for this earthen behemoth. Gophers did, however. Happily scratching and gnawing away inside the dike for months, by early January the rodent holes had weakened the dike so much it breached, sending the swollen Tualatin's waters back out over about 1,000 acres.

Finally now, 140 years after attempts to drain the lake began, man still has not wrestled the beast into complete submission, and he has all but decided to give up trying.

About 30 years after Joseph Gaston came along, another visionary arrived in the area. August Lovegren didn't stay in Gaston, however, and instead headed toward the forked mountain, to the far end of Patton Valley, where he found the ideal spot for his utopian town of Cherry Grove. The townsite had everything Lovegren was looking for except for one thing: a deep lake. He needed a pond to store logs for his lumber mill, but he wanted more than a simple logging pond. He wanted a lake like the ones he swam in as a child in his native Sweden. He wanted the children of his workers to enjoy that same refreshing exercise in Cherry Grove.

A mill pond would have been easy to build, but the lake Lovegren envisioned would take a lot more work. So in 1911, while folks in Gaston were waging their battle to drain Wapato Lake, work began to create a new lake in Cherry Grove, one big enough to swim in. For two years railcars hauled in tons of concrete as workers erected a massive dam across the Tualatin. By September 1913 the dam was finished and the lake began to rise behind it, quickly rising enough to support Lovegren's log booms. By the summer of 1914, it would be big enough for children to swim in.

Sadly the children never got that chance. It rained heavily in the winter of 1913-14. The dam held back the rains of November, and then those of December. By early January the lake already was at its full volume and the rains turned even heavier. Within a few days the lake had turned into a monster, raging against the bedrock that held the dam in place. The bedrock couldn't hold its ground. The dam was breached. The weight of the water and the log boom ripped the dam apart and flooded the town. Lovegren had been enticed to the Gaston area by dreams of a grand lake but now that dream, like his dream of building a timber empire, lay in ruins at his feet. All that was left of his lake was a large empty hole.

Back down on the shores of what once was Wapato Lake, life followed its normal routines. The rains came in October and flooded the fields. The summer sun evaporated the water and yielded the year's onion crop in the 1,000 or so acres the lake once covered. Each year, however, the strains of development grew, and more people meant more demand for food from the area's farmland.

Enter yet another group of visionaries, including a farmer named Henry Hagg. Hagg and a bunch of his friends needed water to irrigate their lands. The Tualatin River watershed benefits from western Oregon's abundant rainfall and always had provided enough water to meet the needs of everyone until the 1960s, when Hagg and associates identified the area's greatest need: A lake. And not just any lake. This one had to hold enough water to irrigate crops and to provide drinking water. Plus, Hagg and company shared Lovegren's dream of a lake deep enough to swim in.

What once had been Wapato Lake did not provide the answer to this need. The land there was too flat and too many homes had been built in the area to make a lake viable. The Tualatin River still flowed freely from the site of Lovegren's folly through the Patton Valley and into Gaston, but the river's bounty had lured some wealthy and prominent people to the valley, so creating a lake there posed many political hurdles. Plus there was the whole issue of unstable bedrock, so another dam in Patton Valley likely would leave us with nothing but another empty hole like the one foretold in the Indian legend. Or the one left by August Lovegren.

So from the mostly dry bed of Wapato Lake in Gaston, Hagg looked past the empty hole of Lovegren's dream, and up and over the next ridge to the place of his dreams, a place that could hold a lake large enough to feed the needs of industry and provide a place for children to swim. He set his sights on Scoggins Valley.

Hagg and associates came up with a plan to build a dam across the valley. The dam would be west of the mighty Stimson Lumber Company's property so as to not disturb the mill's operation, yet at a point where it could capture all of the flow from Scoggins, Sain and Tanner creeks. By 1975 the dam was completed, built to engineering standards August Lovegren never could have imagined 60 years earlier. Scoggins Dam created majestic Henry Hagg Lake, which fed the irrigation needs of Gaston-area farmers, the drinking water needs of thousands and, unlike any local lake before it, the recreational needs of everyone who could drive to its shores.

So about 100 years after Joseph Gaston tried to drain one lake and August Lovegren created and lost another, the Gaston area finally had a lake that could meet every need. Everyone lived happily ever after. Well, not ever after, but for about 25 years. This is not a fairy tale, after all. This is real life in the American West, and there never is enough water in the American West, even in and around soggy Gaston.

Thirsty for more water for drinking, irrigation and recreation, people again are looking to Scoggins, Sain and Tanner creeks for answers. Doubling the height of the dam would provide enough water for future needs, experts say, except that there is no way those three puny little creeks could ever fill a reservoir twice the height of the current one.

Insatiable thirst can drive men to extraordinary measures, and extraordinary measures will be necessary to double the dam. Plans call for water to be pumped back uphill from the Tualatin River downstream from the Scoggins watershed during the winter to fill the lake, only to be released back into the Tualatin in the summer. The released water will make its way downstream to the same place it was pumped out of the river months before, where it will be pumped out again, this time for irrigation needs.

Confused? Well, I warned you right from the start that this story was scary. Scarier still? This little dance of circular logic makes perfect sense to those who have observed Gaston's tangled relationship with water over the years.

A different sort of circle dance is taking place where our story began, back at Wapato Lake. More than 140 years after attempts to tame the lake began, efforts are underway to restore it to its natural state.

Things have changed in 140 years. For example, we don't need so much farmland around Gaston because we can import onions and other produce from all over the world, usually for less than it costs to grow it in places like Gaston.

At the same time, some things haven't changed since the days of Joseph Gaston. Every year, for example, the region still is hit with floods. Ever-denser population and soaring costs are making artificial flood-control methods prohibitive or downright impossible, so experts increasingly are returning to nature's original method of flood-control: swampy, marshy wetlands. Too shallow to swim in or to sustain industry, the wetlands were useless to our forebears, who either drained them or disdained them and went in search of bluer horizons. Today many experts see salvation in the return of a swampy Wapato Lake.

But again I must apologize. None of this has anything to do with the scary monster story passed down through generations by the indigenous people of the area, captured in an obscure, scholarly volume called *Kalapuya Texts*. It

17

seems that the Kalapuya people were content to live for centuries with just the water the spirits gave them. Any hopes for bluer horizons that they might have harbored were disguised in strange legends about water monsters.

So where were we? The story started with something about the footprints of the monster still being visible in Gaston today, blah, blah, blah ... Oh, and then the Water Being dug a slough and drained Wapato Lake, went and dug a lake in what we now call Cherry Grove, but the Water Being was ineffectual and left only a hole ... nothing scary in any of that ... Oh, but wait! We left off with the father hearing the haunting cries of his children from what we now call Scoggins Valley. "We are different!," the children insisted, "Different!"

So anyway, the father climbs down into the valley and finds his children, happily swimming in the lake the Water Being had created in what we call Scoggins Valley, home of Hagg Lake! Finally, a lake deep enough to swim in! Long story short, the kids wanted to stay and play in the lake so Dad went home empty-handed. That's about it. Dad didn't wrestle with the monster, or shoot it and mount its head on the wall ... nothing. Pretty tame stuff. Not really scary, and it doesn't even have a moral to the story. No offense to the Kalapuya, but that's a weird legend. They were right about one thing, however. We really are different now, different in so many ways.

For one thing, we create much scarier water monster stories. Their Water Being dug a trench at Wapato Lake and never looked back; in our story, generations of men wrestled to drain an unruly lake that just keeps rising again and again from the dead to haunt us. Now that's a scary story. Their Water Being made a lake in Cherry Grove but it never even filled up; in our story the Cherry Grove lake did fill up … only to violently destroy a Utopian dream. Scary, right? Their Water Being created a perfectly nice little lake in Scoggins Valley and then was content to swim around forever; in our story, we create a perfectly nice little lake in Scoggins Valley but our insatiable thirst for more and more and more water is *never* satisfied …

Sorry, Kalapuya folks, but you're just not very good storytellers. We are different now. For one thing, we know how to come up with *really* scary ideas. We are different.

Joe Gaston, Abe Lincoln and the Slave Woman

Long before he ever laid eyes on what would become the town of Gaston, Joseph Gaston was a journalist of some repute in his native Ohio. Among his scoops was a story involving Abraham Lincoln and the slave trade, which he recounted in a November 22, 1908, story for *The Oregonian*.

While Gaston was covering Lincoln's presidential campaign he struck up a conversation with the candidate about a mutual friend, a man named Benjamin Cowen. What followed, we're told, is this story about Lincoln's friendship with Cowen many years before.

"While Cowen was a member of Congress in 1842," Gaston wrote in the 1908 story, "Cowen told (Lincoln) he was going to the slave auction to see 'the sum of all villainies' in the deepest hell of its crime against humanity – the sale of a slave advertised as a beautiful woman nearly white, to be carried South in chains to life-long slavery and enforced prostitution. 'I told Cowen,' said Lincoln, 'if you can stand such a sight, you are stronger stuff than I am made of.'"

Cowen did go to the auction and, according to Lincoln's account, got so caught up in the emotions of the proceedings that he began to bid on the woman and kept raising the ante. When the auctioneer slammed his gavel, Cowen was the winner with a bid of $1,100 ... several hundred dollars more than he had with him that day. Upon

20

learning that Cowen was a member of Congress, the slave trader allowed him to take the woman on credit. Cowen went to Lincoln for a loan to cover the balance; instead, Lincoln gave him the money outright.

"This story was news to everyone present but myself," Gaston related. "I had heard Judge Cowen relate it after he had brought the woman back to Ohio and set her free, and where I had often seen her, a comely, capable woman, a useful member of society."

Within months of covering Lincoln's campaign, Joseph Gaston left Ohio for Oregon. Soon his days as a journalist were over, and he settled on a hill overlooking Wapato Lake. He no longer cared much for politics; he had a new swampy quagmire to worry about.

Killer Cows and Cannibals: A Boy's Life in Gaston

Staff Jennings was born in Gaston in 1900.

When he died in 1968 his obituary chronicled in great detail his rise to become one of Portland's best-known businessmen. The obituary skipped over his Gaston years, however, and that's unfortunate, because it would have read like a 1930s serial of a young boy's Wild West adventures, including love triangles, a shootout with a sheriff's posse, suicide, killer cows and perhaps – just perhaps – murder.

Staff Jennings witnessed all that in Gaston before his eighth birthday. By the time he was 18 he could add cannibalism to his list of life experiences.

Generations of Portlanders knew the name Staff Jennings, if for no other reason than that it was emblazoned in giant red letters on the side of a building under the Sellwood Bridge. The building housed the headquarters of his wildly successful company that built and sold boats. By the time he died in 1968, his company had branches throughout the Northwest. His rise was an American Dream worthy of a Horatio Alger story.

Like so many people of his era in Wild West towns like Gaston, Staff Jennings was a first-generation American. His parents, Harold and Mary, had arrived from England just a few years before he was born. Harold gave up his life of sailing the world on cargo ships to settle down as a farmer. Harold and Mary tended farms owned by others as they

22

worked their way up the Coast from California, accompanied at each stop by a dear friend, Robert Wood.

Robert Wood also came to America from England and lived with Harold and Mary wherever they went. When the Jennings decided to buy their own farm, they selected a modest little place on a hill, just across Wapato Lake from Gaston. Robert Wood put up half the money to buy the farm and settled in with the Jennings in the small farmhouse.

Tending farm and raising a small child is a lot of work; more, in fact, than Harold and Mary Jennings and their friend Robert Wood could handle, so they hired a farm hand named Allen George "Harry" McDonald. This is where the plot thickens, where the Horatio Alger story begins to look more like a rock 'em, sock 'em soap opera full of cliffhangers to keep moviegoers coming back for more.

If Harry McDonald had been a character on the movie screen, he would have worn a black hat. Harry was new to Gaston, but he quickly earned a reputation as a barroom brawler and rumors began to fly that he was on the run from California after murdering a man. Despite the rumors, the Jennings hired Harry McDonald to work on the farm alongside Harold and Robert. Harry had a hard time concentrating on his work, however, because he couldn't keep his eyes off Staff Jennings' beautiful young mother, Mary. Quickly tiring of Harry's amorous advances toward his wife, Harold Jennings fired him.

Harry drowned his sorrows in Gaston's saloons, consumed with a jealous rage and thoughts of Staff Jennings' mom across the lake in that little farmhouse. His jealousy, however, was not directed at Harold, but rather at

Robert Wood. Harry McDonald was sure that Robert and Mary were engaged in a torrid love affair. On the evening of July 2, 1905, after a long day of drinking whiskey in town, Harry grabbed a gun and set out to the Jennings' farmhouse to kill Robert Wood. When he arrived at the Jennings' place, Harry leveled the gun at Wood, and then grabbed Mary and started marching her at gunpoint up and down the dirt road in front of the farm as 5-year-old Staff watched in horror.

Finally word of the unfolding drama reached Gaston's town marshal, Charles Wescott, who in turn sent word to the county sheriff in Hillsboro to raise a posse and then raced to the scene along with a couple other townfolk, including Harry Russell. By the time the men got there, McDonald was in the house, where Russell encountered him in the stairwell and ordered him to drop his weapon. Shots were exchanged and Russell retreated, suffering powder burns on his face from McDonald's assault.

The rest of the marshal's men retreated with Russell and awaited the arrival of legendary Wild West Sheriff John Connell and his reinforcements from the county seat of Hillsboro. While the men waited, Harry McDonald holed up in an upstairs bedroom and wrote a suicide note. "For the Jennings family," the note read, "Good-bye to all." It was pinned to a short treatise titled "Jealousy." Then he tied a string to the trigger of a shotgun, tied the other end to his toe, put the barrel in his mouth and blew off the top of his head. At this point McDonald was quite dead, but when Sheriff Connell finally arrived he entered the room with guns blazing, just in case.

Unrequited love, a suicide note, plenty of witnesses. Case closed, at least for law enforcement types. Perhaps only Robert Wood and Mary know if Harry's wild accusations were true. Wood and the Jennings put the case behind them and went on with their lives in the bucolic farmhouse near Gaston, raising a bright little boy named Stafford and milking their small herd of cows, none of whom had heretofore been accused of homicidal violence.

Over the next few years tongues continued to wag in town about the goings on at the Jennings place, but Stafford entered school and his life returned to that of a normal boy ... at least until the early morning hours of August 17, 1908. According to a story in the next day's *The Oregonian*, "with a hole in his heart, evidently made by some blunt instrument, Robert M. Wood was found dead ... near the barn of H.D. Jennings near Gaston." Only 8 years old, Staff Jennings once again was consumed by drama and death.

This case was not nearly as clear-cut as Harry McDonald's had been three years earlier. For example, when Harold found Wood dead outside his barn, there was no "blunt instrument" to be found. Wood was lying dead with a large hole in his chest that penetrated almost all the way through the middle of his heart. But what had made such a savage wound? By the time police arrived on the scene, Harold Jennings had settled on a suspect in this dastardly deed: one of his dairy cows.

Harold told police that he had not seen a thing, because he was in the kitchen with Mary when all the carnage happened. But he and Wood had tended the farm together for years, so he knew his partner's routine. Robert would grab a big stick he kept in the barn and use it to prod the cows out to pasture for the day. What no doubt happened, Jennings told investigators, is that one of the cows had brushed against the stick, pinning Wood against the wall of the barn and impaling him through the chest.

Simple enough, but the police had questions about this scenario. For example, Wood was not found pinned against a wall of the barn, but rather on his back in a field 30 feet away. But sure enough, Wood's trusty prodding stick was right where Jennings told police they would find it, just inside the barn. About an inch and a half of the stick on one end was covered in blood. But that only raised additional questions. Why didn't any of the cows show any sign of injury? Even as tough as cowhide is, police reasoned, an impact strong enough to shatter two of Wood's ribs and penetrate nearly through his body would have left some mark on the cow, too. Even more disturbing? Why, from such a deep and bloody wound, would only an inch and a half of the stick show any sign of Wood's blood?

Other questions arose as well. How is it that in a town where violent crime is almost non-existent, two gruesome deaths had occurred within three years and a few feet of each other? Were Harry McDonald's accusations true after all? Were Robert Wood and Mary embroiled in a torrid love affair right under Mr. Jennings' nose? Had jealousy once again reared its ugly head? What in the world was going on inside this sleepy little compound on the outskirts of sleepy little Gaston?

"Notwithstanding this former tragedy and its unfavorable implication towards Mrs. Jennings," *The*

Oregonian's obviously skeptical reporter wrote, "her husband declares his relations with Wood were friendly and that there was no jealousy between them. In this statement, Jennings is joined by his wife."

Jennings stopped short of denying a relationship might have existed, however, and even if he wasn't sharing his wife with Wood he was sharing the farm with him, and now it would be all his. Harold Jennings had a lot of explaining to do, although it appears that the press showed more skepticism than the police and prosecutors did.

Within a couple of days, county officials held a news conference at which they hoped to "set at rest all doubts as to the manner in which young Wood met his death." They proceeded to dissect suspicions one by one. First, the cow was innocent. Wood, they determined, had simply stumbled while walking with the stick and impaled himself with it as he fell. There was blood only on the tip of the stick, they said, because the wound was "impinging," blocking the flow of blood while it was inside Wood's chest. Wood had pulled the stick from his body himself, they continued, and only when the stick was no longer impinging the arteries did the blood really begin to flow. The clincher? The discovery of a clot of blood inside one of Wood's chest muscles, "proving conclusively that the wound was made before death. Had this wound been inflicted after death this clot would not have formed, this being one of the oldest of facts known to medical science."

The officials did not explain how any of this proved that the impaling was accidental or that Wood had been the one to pull the stick from his chest, but they stressed repeatedly that all this cleared Mr. and Mrs. Jennings of any wrongdoing. "This virtually sets at rest any suspicions that might have been directed against anyone who could have been interested in the removal of Wood," *The Oregonian* concluded. Virtually.

The inquest satisfied authorities, but the public kept buzzing with speculation. Rumors were so pervasive that Harold Jennings felt compelled to write a long letter to *The Oregonian* protesting his innocence and recounting his love for Robert Wood. As evidence, Harold said that Robert Wood's younger brother was, at that very moment, on a ship in the Atlantic, coming to live with him, Mary and young Staff. Despite his protests, the rumors continued and soon Harold and Mary pulled their son out of Gaston schools and moved to Southeast Portland. It's there that Census takers in 1910 recorded the Jennings household, which, sure enough, still included Robert Wood's younger brother, Owen, who arrived by ship from England soon after his brother's death.

So by the age of 10, Staff Jennings' Wild West adventures in Gaston were over. The next installment of his soap-opera life would unfold an ocean away, off the coast of Guam. And this time, the mystery and intrigue would bring him worldwide fame.

When World War I broke out, Harold Jennings decided to put his seafaring skills to use for his adopted country by joining the Merchant Marines. His then 18-year-old son, Stafford, accompanied his father in search of adventure on the high seas. Father and son were assigned to the crew of a wooden merchant ship for its maiden voyage from Portland to Guam. The ship had a connection to their old stomping grounds, being made as it was from green Douglas fir cut from the hills west of Gaston. The ship didn't get very far, however, because after the First Lady, the wife of President Woodrow Wilson, christened the *Dumaru* at Swan Island it slid off the drydock, shot across the Willamette River and hit several houseboats on the other shore. The damage quickly repaired, the *Dumaru* promptly ran aground again before making it out of the Portland harbor. Then, after navigating the stomach-churning trip over the treacherous Columbia River Bar, the *Dumaru* was on its way to San Francisco, but its troubles were far from over.

As it left the cold waters of the Columbia and headed south, the hot sun began to beat down on the green timbers from Gaston, drying them out and causing them to shrink, which in turn caused water to seep into the seams along the boat's hull. The crew frantically bailed water the whole way to San Francisco Bay, and talk of mutiny began. Things went from bad to worse when they arrived at port and learned what their cargo would be in this seemingly jinxed creaky, leaky ship: gasoline and dynamite. This was too much for about half the crew, who chose conscription into the trenches of France over a trip across the Pacific in a ticking time bomb. Staff Jennings and his dad were not among them; they had signed up for this mission and vowed to follow through on their commitment. They soon set sail, no doubt wondering what else could possibly go wrong.

Other things did go wrong on this maiden voyage. Very wrong. Just how wrong is summed up in the title of a best-selling book by famed newsman Lowell Thomas: *"The*

Wreck of the Dumaru: A Story of Cannibalism in an Open Boat."

Not to spoil Thomas's ending, but the *Dumaru* got to within about 20 miles of Guam when it was caught in a storm and struggled toward port. Before they could make it, a huge bolt of lightning struck the ship and the wooden vessel full of explosives burst into flames. Harold Jennings was thrown from the deck of the ship into the raging seas. Heroic Staff Jennings leaped into the waves and pulled his father to the safety of a lifeboat, where they drifted with other survivors for more than two weeks awaiting rescue. It was on this lifeboat that Harold Jennings' amazing life ended when he died of starvation and thirst. He was buried at sea, but not eaten by survivors as Thomas and some of the surviving crew members allege a couple of his crewmates were.

Staff Jennings eventually washed ashore on a remote island of the Philippines, where he was nursed back to health by an odd assortment of natives and drunken Americans hiding from the war effort. Staff was hailed as one of the few heroes of the sorry episode, although he was hardly rewarded for his efforts. When he finally arrived back in Portland he wasn't given the pay he had been promised, but rather just enough money for a new suit of clothes.

From that humble and tragic Wild West beginning, Staff Jennings got on with the business of chasing the American Dream, catching the wave of the Industrial Revolution with his burgeoning boat business. Mary Jennings got on with her life as well, carrying on her tradition of taking in men to share her home; this time another survivor of the *Dumaru*. Mary next made the newspaper in 1951 when she was featured for having become an accomplished swimmer … after overcoming her lifetime fear of water. Staff Jennings' name appeared often after that: most notably in those larger-than-life red letters under the Sellwood Bridge, but also in numerous stories about his adventures aboard the *Dumaru* in the South Seas.

His name never appeared in a story of his adventures in Gaston. His connection to the little farmhouse is traceable only through a painstaking search of Census records and ship manifests. No official record seems to exist of his early days in Gaston, where the true Wild West Adventures of Staff Jennings all began.

A Fleshy Woman
Who Fell in a Well

An 1893 story from *The Oregonian* illustrates how little journalism of the Wild West resembles the milquetoast newspaper stories of today. It also illustrates how different today's workplace is from the days of the Wild West.

The headline, "Fell in a Well," might conjure images of a lighthearted, even humorous, story. But then there's the subhead: "Accidental Death of a Hotel Proprietress in Gaston."

We know little of the subject of the story; not even her first name. We know only that her name was "Mrs. Maytod," and that she had a husband and two daughters. OK, in fairness, we also know that Mrs. Maytod was "a fleshy woman," a detail added by the helpful reporter to explain why she happened to fall through the flimsy cover on a 40-foot-deep well used to supply the hotel with water.

We also know that Mrs. Maytod was inspecting the property with the hotel's owner at the time of her untimely demise, and that the owner faced no further scrutiny for the incident. This was, after all, long before the days of OSHA or other workplace protections.

But of Mrs. Maytod, the fleshy woman with two suddenly motherless daughters, we know little. We know from *The Oregonian*'s account that "within 10 minutes the unfortunate woman was taken from the well, but life was extinct." Presumably life went on for her widower and daughters. There was no such thing as worker's compensation or other workplace protections, but life went on.

Perhaps her widower married a widow, left penniless after her logger husband was killed in the woods. Perhaps he quickly married off his daughters to local suitors.

We don't know, because those details would have only complicated an otherwise simple tale of a fleshy woman who fell in a well.

God Surrounds
a Whistlestop

Gaston never has been known as a particularly pious place.

True to its whistlestop origins, the town has seen its share of raucous Saturday nights that left the good townfolk too tired to attend church the next morning. Sometimes Gaston seems to have relished its reputation for rowdiness; for example, after the local doctor was arrested for selling liquor during Prohibition, the city rallied around him and elected him mayor.

Of course there always have been religious folk in Gaston as well, including the town's founder, Joseph Gaston. Old Joe was married to a particularly righteous woman, and one of his many gifts to the town was a church, which he left to the community when he moved to Portland. Joe didn't return to Gaston very often after he left, and when he did he saw the muddy mess he had left at Wapato Lake and his faltering railroad that formed the town's spine.

We don't know if his personal failures in Gaston bothered him on his return trips, but we do know that he was offended that the ungrateful townfolk he left behind were derelict in what he saw as their duty to the Lord. He was so offended by the condition of his church building that he sued the people to whom he had entrusted its care. He then gave them the deed and washed his hands of it.

Although by and large the lives of early Gaston residents were not ruled by religious doctrine, they soon were surrounded by people for whom religion meant everything.

First came the Seventh-day Adventists in 1904. The Reverend R.M. Airey and his friends chose the Gaston area as the perfect spot for a religious community and residential Academy built on the principles of Christ, clean living and hard work. They did not choose Gaston proper, however, with its hard-living railroad and timber workers. Instead they settled on a secluded little valley five miles southeast of town, past the remnants of Wapato Lake and past Almoran Hill's stagecoach station, in an area they called Laurelwood. Before long, Laurelwood rivaled Gaston in size.

Laurelwood grew steadily but slowly around the Adventist Academy. Over the decades it developed a small merchant and industrial base, both tied directly to the church, which was the center of the community. Throughout its history, Laurelwood has been a humble testament to living in harmony with nature. It still is, although most of its current residents are not members of the church. The fact that Laurelwood remains unincorporated also is testament to its Adventist heritage. At a worldwide gathering of Adventists in Portland, W.F. Martin made his church's feelings toward religion's role in government known: "The lowest ebb of the church ever reached was when it was united with the state; the worst condition of the state was when it was dominated by the church." The Adventists never flexed their considerable muscle in the area, and Laurelwood remains today a quiet, peaceful, mostly vegetarian enclave, all by choice, not by mandate.

Seven years after the Adventists staked their claim five miles southeast of Gaston, the Swedish Baptists set their sights on an area five miles northwest of town, in an area they named Cherry Grove. In contrast to Laurelwood, Cherry Grove's birth was anything but humble. August Lovegren envisioned a boom town of devout, industrious people. A born-again Baptist, Lovegren loved nature as the Adventists did, but his goal was not so much to live in harmony with it as to harness it. Cherry Grove did boom, and within a few short years it had eclipsed both Gaston and Laurelwood, even Forest Grove, boasting a railroad, a thriving lumber mill, multiple hotels and stores of many kinds along its wooden sidewalks. By 1913 it even had electricity, produced by a mammoth concrete dam across the Tualatin River. In three short years, Cherry Grove was on a trajectory to outshine all of the older cities in Washington County. But three years is about all the longer Lovegren's dream survived and today all that remains of it is ruins and a street that bears his name. All commerce is gone. Soon the abandoned school will be gone, too, after the county manages to rid it of the squatters who inhabit it, cooking on open fires inside the building. His church remains, too, perhaps most famous for its role as host to one of 20th-Century America's most famous con men, who spent time there as pastor.

August Lovegren's devout faith is what prompted him to leave his native Sweden for America, his daughter Mabel wrote in the 1970s. He left in search of a place to start over after his father disowned him for the grievous sin of converting from Methodist to Baptist. He amassed a fortune when he built a mill near Seattle to produce shingles for the buildings and homes rising during the city's boom. But not content to simply participate in a town's rise to prosperity, Lovegren decided he wanted to create a city of his own. Patton Valley fit the bill perfectly as a canvas for his dreams.

The spot he chose is at the wilderness end of the valley, where the Tualatin River rapids drop from the Coast Range to create the broad, flat farmland that stretches to the business end of the valley at Gaston. Starting about a mile east of the townsite and for the rest of its meandering journey to the Willamette River, the Tualatin is a flat, slow, murky stream, productive as an irrigation source but otherwise of little importance except when it overflows its banks and causes destruction. At its headlands, however, the Tualatin is a wild, rugged river flanked by towering Douglas firs and yews. The headlands reminded Lovegren of his childhood home in Sweden, Mabel tells us, and perhaps even of his childhood itself.

Young August, Mabel writes, left school at age nine to earn money for his family. Without education or culture, August weaved a life for himself in the wilderness of Sweden, hauling bricks and enduring a slave-like apprenticeship with the village blacksmith. He careened through life until one day when his course was forever altered after he stopped by a Bible group to meet new people. The Bible stopped him in his tracks. Although still industrious, August felt a sudden stillness come over his soul.

After coming to America, Lovegren again made his way through the wilderness, eventually creating the shingle mill near Seattle that begat the rough-and-tumble town of Preston. Still, his ambition was tempered from that day he met the Bible, and he felt the pressure building to create something more meaningful, something more in line with his image of an ideal world. The untamed stretch of the Tualatin was just the spot.

After settling on his townsite, Lovegren moved with lightning speed to realize his dream. In December of 1910 he introduced his concept in the Forest Grove *News-Times*, which headlined its exclusive "Epoch of Development is Unsurpassed in County's Annals." The town would include fountains, paved sidewalks, and, even more impressive, "electricity will be used to illuminate the town."

The first step was a spur to connect with the rail line near Gaston. To accomplish that, Lovegren had to create his own company, which he named the Willamette Valley and Coast Railroad. The founding fathers of Gaston were nervous about all of Lovegren's development and after about 40 years as an unincorporated village they began creating formal services, such as a town marshal and a fire department, each of which came to fruition in 1913, a year before Gaston's official incorporation was accepted by the state of Oregon. They had no way of knowing that by the time the articles of incorporation were accepted, Cherry Grove would lie in ruins.

The Lovegren Lumber Company opened a sawmill in 1911 and started turning out lumber to finance August's grander dreams, which he believed would be realized by his

Cherry Grove Land Company. In the meantime, Lovegren worked tirelessly to harness the power of the wild Tualatin. Work began on a huge concrete dam at a point upriver that seemingly offered a secure footing in bedrock. The dam would create electricity for the rugged outpost and a holding pond for the large rafts, or "booms," of lumber floated to the mill from the forest lands of the Coast Range. The dam would accomplish something else as well; it would create a lake of the sort Lovegren knew in Sweden, one in which townspeople could relax and enjoy their wilderness home.

The centerpiece of Lovegren's dream would take time to build. Timber from the mill was used to build forms into which tons of concrete were poured. But November of 1912 produced a Democratic Congress, a Congress Lovegren felt was beholden to the needs of the East Coast elite and out of touch with the spirit of the American West. Sure enough, the Democrats overturned tariffs on wood imported from Canada, which Lovegren blamed for a sudden drop in demand for his lumber. Lovegren already had endured many boom and bust cycles in his career, so he knew how to ride out the storm. As angry as he was at the Democrats we can assume he never used the Lord's name in vain, and instead he dipped into his ample reserves to undercut the prices of his competitors.

Lovegren's religious fervor spurred him on to build a large Baptist church that still stands today as the only remaining public legacy to his grand vision. He built tennis and croquet courts and a beautiful baseball diamond for the children of the community, all the while remaining ahead of similar efforts in Gaston and Laurelwood. Still, his focus remained on a dream grander in scale than any harbored in those nearby villages, a dam that would harness the Tualatin for the good of mankind. For three years, ton upon ton of concrete went into the makings of that dream.

Downriver in Gaston, civic leaders debated arcane articles of incorporation. Further east, dreamers in Laurelwood plowed fields and made plans for a factory in which students of the Academy could handcraft furniture to pay for their education and learn the value of physical labor. The Adventists didn't have a river to dam, but that wouldn't have been their style anyway. The peaceful, vegetarian Adventists just wanted to appreciate and live in harmony with nature.

Upriver, Lovegren's dream continued to grow. He called upon his bankers, and he called upon his business acumen, and he called upon the true believers who had followed him to his promised land. Most of all, he called upon his faith. Democrats be damned; soon the wild Tualatin would be dammed in Jesus' name … and August Lovegren would be one *very* rich man.

Throughout 1911 and 1912 the massive concrete dam rose. Lumber rolled down the rail line to just north of Gaston, bypassing the town and its struggling mills. By September 1913, Lovegren's crews were finished with the dam. With the Tualatin at its lowest ebb of the year, the gates were shut, awaiting the winter rains to fill the reservoir.

The water rose quickly. Farmers in the lower Patton Valley and in the slumbering town of Gaston might have suffered from lack of water, but Lovegren's log booms accumulated in the still waters behind the dam. Decades after the white man settled in the area, finally someone had captured the region's potential. With nature conquered, Lovegren continued his quest to conquer the demons that held back men from realizing their full potential.

Fueled by his faith in God, Lovegren had been able to create a utopian future for his fellow man that had eluded contemporaries in Gaston and Laurelwood. His bold action had bested Gaston in its secularism and Laurelwood in its search for balance with the world around it.

Lovegren had overcome secularism and the naïve hope for harmony with nature. In three short years he had foreseen the obstacles and he had overcome them. He had overcome every obstacle anyone could throw in the path of a devout, brilliant-but-uneducated child of the American miracle. He had achieved the promise God made to him back in Sweden.

The people of Gaston lacked such vision. The community grew from a couple hundred settlers in the 1870s to a population of 221 in the 1920 Census, its first official count after incorporating in 1914. In the next decade the city grew by only six people. While the growth rate accelerated somewhat, by 2010 Gaston still counted only a little more than 600 souls.

The founders of Laurelwood also had a vision they inherited from God, but that vision never panned out exactly as they thought it would. The community saw slow but steady growth until societal forces conspired to doom the residential school. In 2004, exactly a hundred years after it was founded, the Academy was gone, although the community that grew up around it remains.

Yet while the founders of Gaston and Laurelwood lacked a grand vision, they did understand that it rains a lot in western Oregon and that most of that precipitation falls between September and January. The folks in Gaston understood that fact of nature particularly well, watching Wapato Lake come back to life every fall despite their best efforts to drain it.

By January 1914 Wapato Lake was back almost to its natural state, filled with the rain falling in the valleys. In the hills around Cherry Grove, the precipitation had fallen as several feet of snow. Then a particularly heavy January storm brought a deluge of rain and temperatures warm enough to melt the snowpack. Four months after Lovegren's dam went into service on the Tualatin, that storm created a problem that neither Lovegren nor, apparently, God could overcome.

The reservoir was filled and a large boom of logs was resting against the dam, ready to be processed in the mill. The north end of the dam was built on flat land and could have given against the weight of the storm, but it held fast. The south end was not thought to be in jeopardy, embedded as it was in the bedrock channel cut by the river. The natural flow of the river pressed all the accumulated weight of water and logs against that southern side. The dam, two years in the making but until now never tested by the storms of Oregon, gave way. It didn't survive its first winter, and Lovegren's log boom and his dreams were swept away in the current.

Lovegren Lumber was in ruins. The flood created by the dam breach destroyed the hopes of those who had flocked to Cherry Grove. Lovegren blamed the Democrats for his plight and soon surrendered his interest in the now worthless mill to absolve himself of his earthly debt. He kept his interest in the Cherry Grove Land Company but moved back to the Puget Sound area to rebuild his fortune with a shingle mill, boosted by the rising tide of national economic recovery.

Lovegren never saw his utopian dreams materialize in Cherry Grove. Just three years after his dam burst, he died of stomach cancer in Seattle. Even if he had lived he would have been disappointed. Without the dam and mill to sustain it, the Cherry Grove Land Company was not worth much.

Once a pioneer in rural electrification, after the dam breach Cherry Grove would go without power for decades until Franklin Roosevelt's push to electrify rural America once again illuminated its homes. The hotels and other businesses closed up shop until by the 1980s there were no services in the town. By the time the last store closed, Cherry Grove was as well-known for its criminal element as it was for its scenic beauty and long-forgotten religious roots.

Laurelwood's story lacks the drama of Cherry Grove's, without either boom or bust. The original Academy closed in 1984 and the property nearly took a decidedly non-utopian turn several times. In 1985, for example, it almost became the Oregon Police Academy until the state decided to expand the campus at Monmouth. A few years later it was eyed as a site for a minimum-security prison. Eventually another group of Adventists managed to reopen it as a boarding school, but that dream died too, in 2004. One hundred years after the Academy's founding all that remained of its founders' dreams were vacant buildings and aging neighbors who had studied and/or worked at the school. Utopia had bypassed the slopes of Bald Peak, as well. Until 2011 ...

In 2011, 100 years after Cherry Grove's founding, new religious life flowed into Laurelwood. The Ananda religious community purchased the old Academy campus with an eye toward creating a worldwide spiritual retreat. With a philosophy of harmony with nature, the Anandans' worldview nearly mirrors the Adventists'. The community's leaders talk of bringing new commerce into Laurelwood, but slowly and on a sustainable scale.

God has not always delivered on what his followers believed to be his promises for the Gaston area, but that has not stopped his followers from believing. Lovegren's Cherry Grove church still stands, as does Joseph Gaston's. Now with the Anandans, God's followers feel a new groundswell of hope, and once again the epicenter is Gaston.

Well, not Gaston exactly, but close enough for the Almighty to keep an eye on old Joe's neglected, rundown church in the whistlestop he founded.

An Unlikely Battlefield for Class Warfare

The first wave of the Industrial Revolution went pretty much unnoticed in Gaston.

While others flocked to Detroit and Pittsburgh and Akron and elsewhere to work in factories, the people of Gaston went on doing what they always had done: working in the fields and forests or running small stores catering to the agrarian workers. No one got rich, but few people starved, either. The gap between the richest and poorest of Gaston's population was surprisingly small. Doctors, merchants, farmers, loggers ... everyone knew everyone and everyone knew everyone else had to work hard to make a living.

In short, Gaston seemed to be about the unlikeliest town in America for class warfare, at least until C.W. Stimson and the Sawmill and Timber Workers Union came to town. Even then tensions stayed beneath the surface, if just barely, until a rich, aristocratic old Army general named Charles H. Martin got involved.

When "Old Iron Pants," as Martin's World War I troops called him, entered the picture as Oregon Governor, Gaston exploded into violence that sent shockwaves across the Northwest and helped alter the state's political landscape for decades.

Just as the stock market was about to crash in 1929, Stimson, one of the West Coast's biggest timber barons, decided on a spot just north of Gaston to build the lumber mill to end all lumber mills. On October 9, 1933, the state-of-the-art mill in Scoggins Valley began operations, bringing much-needed jobs to Gaston. Just two years later it brought some of the worst labor violence in Oregon history.

C.W. Stimson was, according to a book his company commissioned, beloved by his workers, as was the man he chose to lead the new Gaston operation, son-in-law Harold Miller. Miller, like Stimson (but unlike nearly anyone in his new home of Gaston), had been born into luxury. He was born far from Gaston in Detroit, Michigan, and his family had, among other things, created the town of Concrete, Washington (named for the family's huge cement company). As a child, Miller moved with his father to Aberdeen when his father branched into the lumber business.

John Ross and Margaret Byrd Adams, the authors the Stimson company commissioned to write its history in the 1983 book *The Builder's Spirit*, assure us that the Stimson and Miller families engendered fierce loyalty among the highly paid and well-cared-for workers they employed. Yet even in this fawning book there are signs that not all was so rosy. As a boy, Harold was pulled from his job at his father's Aberdeen Lumber mill, according to the authors, "to keep him away from the saws that too often cost even experienced workers their hands and fingers." His father took that precaution despite the fact that Harold, unlike those unlucky workers he employed, would have lived comfortably after losing a hand in the mill.

Another passage from the book offers a glimpse into the management style Miller learned at his father's side. In

46

The Builder's Spirit, we learn this about Miller's young life in his family's company-owned town of Concrete: "With its population of rowdy workers, it was not an ideal town in which to raise a family. Ernest (Harold's father) carried brass knuckles and a revolver for protection" from his own employees. In fact, the authors go on to explain, Miller "removed one angry worker from his home through the front window."

By 1933, Harold Miller had graduated from Stanford University and married C.W.'s daughter, Jane, making him heir to an even greater fortune than his father's. They settled into a home across Scoggins Valley Road from the Gaston mill to start their lives together. Soon, we're told, "Trust and understanding between the Millers and the mill employees created a productivity and a loyalty that was the envy of the industry." The Stimson workers demonstrated that loyalty time and again, even risking their lives to go into the forest to battle the Tillamook Burn for their employer, although the fawning biographers acknowledge that some of the workers "went berserk" in the raging inferno "and had to be locked in a tool shed" by Stimson bosses. Still, the authors assure us, there was no class warfare between the Stimsons and Millers and the "proud, simple dedicated people of pioneer stock" they employed in Gaston.

We're told that the Stimsons and Millers downplayed their wealth, although Jane Stimson Miller later recalled a favorite quote from her grandmother: "They always grumble that the lumber business is never any good, but I've always worn a silk petticoat." By all accounts Jane tried to not let the family's silk petticoats, yachts and lavish estates up and down the West Coast prevent her from fitting in with the people of Gaston, many of whom still lacked electricity and indoor plumbing. In fact, the Millers' own home near the mill lacked electricity when they first came to town.

As much as the Millers and Stimsons sought solidarity with the men who toiled in the mill, it didn't take long for those bonds to be tested. At the depths of the Great Depression and just a little more than a year after the Gaston mill was in full operation, sawmill workers across Oregon went on strike. Desperate for jobs to feed their families but also desperate for humane working conditions, the employees turned to the fledgling unions of the Northwest for protection and representation.

The Gaston mill was among the most modern, cleanest and safest in North America, and its workers did not immediately join their brothers on the picket line. Soon, however, representatives of various unions arrived from Portland and elsewhere to encourage the Gaston crews to become members. Ross and Adams insist that the workers' early hesitation to strike "demonstrated the strength of employee loyalty" to the Stimsons and Millers. Just how strong that loyalty really was remains a matter of debate, but there no doubt were other reasons for the hesitancy.

The agrarian nature of 1930s Gaston meant there was little if any history of management-labor disputes. Sons rarely went on strike against their fathers for better working conditions at the family farm, logging operation or general store. Any hardship as a worker would someday pay off in the inheritance of the business. Gaston's culture was one that seems alien to most people from a bustling city such as

Portland or Astoria, but remnants of that culture are alive and well even today. There are many people around Gaston and Cherry Grove who don't have traditional jobs or careers but who manage to survive on the occasional odd job.

In many cases, these people have inherited a home or a small plot of land and a self-reliant jack-of-all-trades set of skills from their parents. They stock their freezers with elk shot during hunting season and salmon caught in the Trask or Wilson rivers and manage to eke out a living doing odd jobs, perhaps welding, mowing fields, cutting firewood, repairing tractors or selling scrap. If conditions in one of their odd jobs become unbearable they don't go on strike; they simply stop doing that particular chore. Now, as in the 1930s, many in Gaston are not beholden to any corporation or union. On the other hand, many of those who *are* beholden are reliant on the Stimson Lumber Company, which remains by far the area's largest private employer. If they screw up and lose their job at the mill, finding a comparable job can be next to impossible. That creates a kind of loyalty born more out of necessity than affection.

That's not to say that there wasn't at least some genuine affection for the mill's owners, but employees rarely saw C.W. Stimson, who spent much of the Depression sailing his yacht in Puget Sound. Harold and Jane Miller spent their summers in Gaston but wintered in Portland and within a few years packed up and moved to the city for good. Regardless, throughout its history, the Gaston mill has seen little labor discord since those brutal years in the Great Depression. Whatever their role was in the strike, C.W. Stimson and Harold Miller are not the names generally associated with the violence at the mill that became legend in the annals of Northwest labor history during a couple of brutal, Depression Era years. That honor goes to proud Army General Charles H. Martin.

Martin loved America and spent many years fighting for it. Sadly, he was much less fond of many of the Americans who inhabited the land he loved so much, and he is better remembered for the years he spent fighting against them.

Martin's story is one of good luck, plodding hard work and a healthy dose of heroism, but also of unapologetic racism and violence against workers struggling to feed their children in the depths of the Great Depression. The violence and racism cannot be dismissed as youthful indiscretions, either, coming as they did at the culmination of a long and distinguished military career paid for with the blood and money of the people he held in such contempt.

Martin graduated from West Point and landed a post at the Vancouver Barracks in the 1880s. There, according to Martin biographer Gary Murrell, his career stalled in mediocrity until he crossed the Columbia River to marry the daughter of Ellis Hughes, one of Oregon's richest and most-powerful men. Soon Martin's career soared until he earned the rank of major general, serving as assistant chief of staff for the Army along the way. He was very much a product of his time, an era of expansionism and exceptionalism.

Martin earned his stars in conflicts – the Boxer Rebellion and the Spanish-American War, for example – that had less to do with defending American lives than with promoting the white Anglo-Saxon Christian interests of

America's large institutions. After his heroic leadership as a World War I general, Martin focused his military career on defending corporate interests at the Panama Canal, where he brutally crushed a peasant revolt. At each stop along the way, Martin did his best to thwart human and civil rights for Americans of color.

Racism was common in the military of the day, just as it was in general society, but Martin's fervor in defending the practice set him apart. Ironically, many of the 350,000 African-Americans who successfully pleaded for their right to defend their country during World War I were sent to serve in France, which is where Martin's command was. He didn't allow most blacks into combat units, but he had a front-row seat as black soldiers gave their lives serving in positions supporting the white soldiers on the front lines. The African-Americans were not immune to the bullets, bombs and flu bugs that killed without prejudice, but they were exempt from Martin's gratitude for helping to make his command so successful. In fact, after the war, Martin was a leader in efforts to thwart equal rights to minorities in the Army. "The negro is of very little importance," he wrote. "The average negro is not by any means equal to the average white man." As reward for his racism he was given command of, and control over, the 92nd Division, which consisted entirely of what were then called "negroes."

But as much as Martin hated blacks, he despised reds even more. In fact his hatred toward people he considered to be communists bordered on paranoia and led to a political demise of tragic proportions, all documented brilliantly in Murrell's *Iron Pants*.

"Old Iron Pants" Martin's long and distinguished military career, plus riches inherited from his in-laws, allowed him to retire in comfort to the place of his choosing. Forsaking his native Illinois, he returned to Oregon, where he inherited his father-in-law's fortune. This was in 1928, before Henry Kaiser's World War II shipyards attracted black workers to Portland, so even more than today Oregon was a good place for Martin to avoid "the average negro." He settled comfortably into a Portland neighborhood and began a second career as a politician. Initially he was as successful in politics as he had been in the military. In a little more than two years in Oregon, he was elected to Congress. He was re-elected two years later and set his sights on bigger things. By March 1935 his new home was the Oregon governor's mansion in Salem.

When he was sworn in, Martin had no way of knowing that after decades of dazzling victories in battles in France that his Waterloo would be the sleepy little town of Gaston. Racism was not his undoing, however, because Gaston was even whiter than Portland. There were, by then, Japanese families working the nearby onion fields, but the faces of Gaston definitely were not black.

Martin's firm belief in Manifest Destiny certainly played a role in his downfall. Fresh off his term as commander of the Panama Canal Zone, his pet project as a member of Congress had been construction of the Bonneville Dam on the Columbia, which he believed would provide electricity to turn Oregon into an industrial powerhouse. Some historians give Martin credit as the prime force behind funding for the dam, but he soon found himself in fierce opposition to how the dam was being operated. Although the devout anti-socialist had used taxpayer money to build the dam, he wanted it handed over to his corporate friends for their personal enrichment. In a precursor to his attack on the workers of Gaston, Martin railed wildly about the "Jew Communists" who advocated for the dam's power to be controlled by people's utility districts and farmer cooperatives.

As governor, Martin turned the state police into his own private investigation unit and co-opted the Portland Police Bureau's "Red Squad" to control his enemies and critics. Martin didn't like anyone getting in the way of what he wanted, and he wanted nothing more than to turn Oregon's lush natural resources into corporate profits. "We turn to our forbears in a sense of deepest reverence and greatest affection," he wrote. "They builded (sic) well. They dominated every element that undertook to thwart their way." Chief among elements Martin wanted to dominate as governor was Oregon's timber, "of which," he said, "we have scarcely availed ourselves." That put the little agrarian town of Gaston squarely in his targets. Oregon's biggest timber barons had selected Gaston as the state's logging headquarters, and Martin was not about to let the area's "proud, simple dedicated people of pioneer stock" ruin things for his out-of-state corporate friends.

Although elected as a Democrat, Martin had little in common with the Democrat in the White House, Franklin Roosevelt. He spoke more fondly of two other world leaders, Benito Mussolini and Adolf Hitler, than he did of the father of the New Deal. In particular, he vehemently objected to the new Department of Labor, which he decried as "Bolshevik" and unconstitutional. Martin had no use for the regulations this bureaucracy wanted to impose, such as interfering with a corporation's right to lock berserk employees in tool sheds when sent in to battle raging infernos with little training or safety equipment. His loyalty was unabashedly with the corporate titans of the day, so when the working-class mill workers across the state went on strike for higher wages and better working conditions, it was no secret whose side Martin was on.

Exactly where most of the workers at the Gaston mill stood on the issue is a little murkier. In May 1935, Stimson was operating after many other mills in the region had been shut by strikers. The Sawmill and Timber Workers union sent pickets to Gaston from Portland, St. Helens, Astoria and elsewhere. Many Gaston workers had walked out, but were promptly replaced with strikebreakers hired by the Stimsons. By sending outside picketers, the union said it was showing support for Stimson workers who wanted to join the union but who were too intimidated to walk out. The authors of *The Builder's Spirit* have a very different take. In this version it was the union doing the intimidating, trying to coerce the remaining Gaston workers to join the strike against their will.

Soon after Stimson hired strikebreakers to keep the mill operating, it hired armed guards. According to Stimson's history, these guards were hired to protect the families of management and to protect the mill's workers from the violent, out-of-control outside agitators. In *The Builder's Spirit*, Martin is portrayed as being immensely patient with the strikers, who, according to the book, were destroying the state's apparently otherwise healthy Depression-era economy (in fact in 1936 Martin declared the Depression at an end in Oregon ... under his leadership the state was, in his estimation, immune to the problems that afflicted the rest of the nation, dragged down only by those pesky union members demanding a living wage). Still, we're told, Martin urged peaceful mediation and ordered the use of police only to protect the workers. Washington County Sheriff John Connell is portrayed as equally reluctant to confront the workers.

The authors tell us that the outside unionists continued acts of violence against the Gaston workers, who hated the big-city union organizers and loved the Millers and Stimsons. Finally fed up, the authors tell us, Martin and Connell were forced to confront the 150-200 pickets with hundreds of state police officers, sheriff's deputies (many deputized just for the occasion), plus Stimson's private army of what the book admits were "vigilantes." Then the pickets were marched the eight miles into Forest Grove, where they were put on trucks and hauled away to jail. There's no mention in these accounts of any violence perpetrated against the pickets. Miller, Stimson, Connell and Martin, the authors want us to believe, were simply standing up for the rights of the workers, who wanted to remain non-union.

Other accounts saw the confrontation from a very different perspective. Other industries were hurting because of the strike, most notably farmers, who were facing a disastrous shortage of crates for the year's berry crop. That particular issue, however, already had been rectified by the

Oregon Federation of Labor, which negotiated an agreement with strikers to produce the needed crates. In addition, strikers already had agreed to industry's two major compromise demands: A 40-hour workweek (up from 35) at 50 cents an hour, down from the 75 cents the union wanted.

This was not enough for Martin, however, as Vernon Jensen points out in his book *Lumber and Labor.* Connell and Martin had warned the strikers to stay off the Scoggins Junction of the Tualatin Valley Highway, and by most accounts the workers complied, but the state and corporate vigilantes attacked anyway, armed with machine guns that Martin had ordered to be used if the strikers resisted.

The machine guns were not used, but newspaper photos show heavily armed police officers beating unarmed strikers with clubs and sticks, some with smiles on their faces and few showing any great reluctance to use force. Nor do most accounts show any reluctance on the part of either Connell or Martin. In fact, early in the strike Martin wrote a letter to the state's sheriffs, and published in *The Oregonian*, ordering them to use violence against strikers to keep the mills open. Some sheriffs were genuinely reluctant to attack their own citizens, including Columbia County Sheriff Oscar Weed, whom Martin publicly ridiculed and threatened to remove from office for his softness.

Infuriated by the strikers' refusal to return to work, Martin had instructed the state's sheriffs to confront the strikers. "Beat the hell out of them," he commanded. "Crack their damned heads. These fellows are there for nothing but trouble … give it to them!" Unlike Weed, Sheriff Connell was happy to oblige, and Gaston became his battlefield of choice.

Martin proudly modeled his resistance to the demands of workers on one of his political heroes, the up-and-coming young leader of Germany. He told several colleagues that Adolf Hitler's brownshirts were an inspiration to him. Murrell cites letters Martin wrote to fellow generals, warning that "this continued prating about human rights being placed above property rights is certainly bearing bitter fruit. I believe eventually (people) will crush it." Again citing Hitler as his role model, Martin asserted that "I don't believe Americans will submit."

Charles Martin's brutality in Gaston emboldened Washington's governor, the unrelated Clarence Martin, to step up his strikebreaking ways and a month later in Tacoma 300 National Guardsmen rained tear gas down on a rally that even the staunchly anti-labor *Seattle Star* acknowledged had "little violence reported" before the tear gas assault.

Despite the crackdown, labor strife continued at the Gaston mill for another two years. Finally in February 1937 the federal government ordered Stimson to allow a vote to see which side the workers really were on. The vote left the workers' wishes murkier than ever. They voted against joining the Sawmill Workers union, but the election hadn't settled the unrest, and another strike shut down the mill. In August, the government ordered yet another vote for these workers who supposedly hated unions. This time they voted to join a different union, the Brotherhood of Carpenters and Joiners. The mill remained union for the next six decades. In the end, Gaston's "proud, simple dedicated people of pioneer stock" were not willing to bend to the demands of either a large corporation or a large union, and instead went their own way.

It's hard to say who won that war in Gaston. The Millers and Stimsons did fine for themselves, becoming even more fabulously wealthy over the decades, dotting the West Coast with mansions and summer retreats. The people of Oregon benefited from that wealth, as the Millers poured much of their fortune into charitable causes. The Stimson Foundation also has given generously to causes large and small across the state. "Peggy," the steam engine that hauled the first lumber from the mill back in the 1930s, is a centerpiece of the World Forestry Center in Portland. Pacific University, the exclusive Catlin Gabel School and many other institutions have benefited from the Stimson presence in Gaston.

Mill workers benefited from the strike as well, with average hourly wages for Washington County sawmill employees rising from 59 cents an hour when the labor unrest began in 1935 to 71 cents, a 20 percent increase, when the plant unionized two years later. Over the next couple of decades, the Stimsons and Millers even handed out raises to their workers that weren't mandated by union contracts.

In the summer of 1975 it appeared trouble was brewing again on the banks of Scoggins Creek. Industry giant Weyerhaeuser and nearly every other Northwest timber company had settled on a contract with their unions, but Stimson was offering much less to its employees. Stimson held firm, arguing that as a company totally reliant on the depressed construction industry it could not compete with Weyerhaeuser, Crown-Zellerbach and other competitors who could switch to buying the cheap logs used in their paper businesses. The trees around Gaston were good, solid timber that didn't come cheap.

Finally one Monday morning in July, defiant union workers walked out. By the next morning, a number of the strikers walked right back in, along with a group of non-union strikebreakers. Striking workers again lined Scoggins Valley Road, taunting those who crossed their picket line. Washington County Sheriff's deputies stood ready along the roadway as well, ready to take action if the scene exploded like it had 40 years earlier.

The stand-off continued for 11 weeks, but this time ended with handshakes rather than handcuffs. The workers ended up with an agreement almost identical to their Weyerhaeuser brethren. Stimson's chief negotiator, Ralph Nordlund, said of the agreement: "We are extremely pleased," he told the *News-Times*, "it has been a difficult time for all concerned." It had not, however, been anywhere near as difficult as in 1935, because now there was a new sheriff in town and, more importantly, a different governor in Salem, each of whom was content to let the good people of Gaston settle their problems on their own terms.

Changes brought about by federal regulations, union rules, technology and a corporate commitment to the safety of workers means that the loss of fingers and hands is no longer common. When accidents do happen, workers are protected by government resources brought about by the New Deal. The Gaston labor scene is returning to its historical ambivalence toward both corporations and organized unions. Within the boundaries of the Gaston fire and school districts, Stimson remains the only major corporate presence; there are not even any fast-food franchises, gas stations or banks.

So in the end, the Stimsons survived the strike of 1935, as did the Miller family, which still runs the company almost 80 years later. So did the workers who have depended on jobs at the mill for generations.

There was just one clear loser in the battle of Scoggins Valley. General Charles Martin's last battle resembled a suicide mission more than it did his successful military campaigns. Arrogantly siding with out-of-state corporations over the common man, he gambled on forsaking the Democratic voters who elected him to instead woo the state's corporate and media heavyweights, who then as now were mostly Republicans. His gamble was a fiasco. He survived an aborted recall attempt, but Democratic voters rejected him in the next primary and Republicans seized on the Democrats' disarray to elect as Governor Charles Sprague, publisher of the *Salem Statesman* and one of the titans of industry Martin had sought to please. It would be 20 years before Democrats could rise from the rubble and recapture Salem. His reputation in ruins, Martin retreated to Portland and lived out his life in the quiet luxury his wife's inheritance afforded him.

Rich, aristocratic Charles Martin had prevailed in battles in China, Panama and France, but he met his Waterloo one day along Scoggins Creek, just up the road from Gaston, a most unlikely place in which to wage class warfare.

Capitalism's Yin and Yang Collide in Gaston

Bitter rivals Joe Gaston and Ben Holladay stand almost as iconic caricatures of the best and worst of the capitalists who built the modern American West.

There's no question into which category most who knew him would place Holladay. "Proper Portlanders were fascinated by his success and repelled by his style of life," wrote Portland State University Professor Carl Abbott in *Portland, Gateway to the Northwest*. "They whispered that he had populated his house with high-priced prostitutes and competed to find the right adjectives to describe him: vulgar, low, haughty, dictatorial, dishonest and immoral were some of the favorites."

Holladay had sold his Pony Express mail service to Wells Fargo and invested his fortune into Oregon steamships and railroads. Backed by Portland's monied establishment, Joseph Gaston had secured rights to build a line from Portland to Salem and on to Eugene with plans to continue on into California. Holladay wanted that route and ended up wresting it away from Gaston. The "low, dishonest and immoral" means he used to achieve that goal included tens of thousands of dollars in bribes to members of the Oregon Legislature.

Joe Gaston was no match for Holladay's deceit and he lost the rights to the lucrative eastside line along the Willamette River. In return he was thrown a veritable crumb: rights to a westside rail line past Wapato Lake and through Wapato Gap, connecting Hillsboro to Corvallis.

Gaston could not have been much more different from Holladay. Well-educated, articulate, with a Puritanical work ethic and outlook on life, Gaston prided himself on his honesty. For example, at one point he fired the entire staff of his railroad. "The reason why," the *Forest Grove Independent* explained, "was that they had been charging passengers two and four bits for small packages, valises, umbrellas, etc., which they had no right to."

Honesty was not always the best policy for insuring success in the Wild West, and soon "rampaging, rapacious, ruthless" Ben Holladay had wrested Gaston's struggling Westside Railroad from him as well. But, then again, rapaciousness isn't always such a wise idea, either. To fuel his thirst to monopolize Oregon's transportation system, Holladay tapped out all the local sources of money and had to borrow from German banks at high interest rates. After taking over Gaston's rail line, Holladay found himself buried in debt he couldn't pay. The German bankers were every bit as ruthless as Holladay, and they snatched away his company, selling it in turn to Henry Villard. Villard's assessment of Holladay after the transaction? "Illiterate, coarse, boastful, false and cunning."

Don't feel bad for Holladay, however. He had lost most of his fortune but still lived in grand style, marrying off his two daughters to European royalty. He died in Portland in 1887, shunned by the city's high society but more than comfortable in his huge house with, perhaps, the prostitutes he supposedly employed.

Joseph Gaston lived for 26 years after his nemesis died, spending most of those years in a house in Portland that was grander even than Holladay's. He was fiercely devoted to his wife and daughter, who rather than marrying royalty lived her entire life with her father, dying days after he did in 1913. In those 26 years, Gaston built several more successful businesses and wrote prolifically about the history of Portland and Oregon.

Joseph Gaston also became a favorite of the Populist Party, although he never actively campaigned for office. The Populists loved him because he epitomized the American Dream, rising from rags to riches without ever forgetting those still left wearing rags.

Joseph Gaston, one of Oregon's most successful entrepreneurs and staunchest supporters of free enterprise, believed that enterprise could be truly free only if democracy allowed the people of the United States to place limits on the powers of corporations. "PEOPLE HAVE POWER," the headline in *The Oregonian* of April 10, 1912, read. "Remedy for Corporate Control," the subhead read. The headlines were on an opinion piece written by Joseph Gaston, a man who could have been written off as bitter for having been bested by multinational corporations and the politicians those corporations corrupt. He probably was bitter; we know he never forgave Ben Holladay, his rival who had died in disgrace so many years before.

Still, as Joseph Gaston wrote those words just months before his own death, he was living very comfortably in one of Portland's biggest homes. He had recovered from Holladay's attacks and rebuilt his fortune, giving him the freedom to write his books about Portland and Oregon. History, it is said, is written by the winners.

Joseph Gaston was one of Oregon's great historians.

A Most Dastardly Attempt

Joseph Gaston did not like his rival railroad tycoon, Ben Holladay, describing him as "wholly destitute of fixed principles of honesty, morality or common decency." Ben Holladay was so ruthless in his quest to monopolize Oregon's transportation systems that it seemed nothing could get in his way.

But Ben Holladay nearly met his untimely demise in April 1873 while riding on his private train through Gaston, a town named for his bitter rival. He nearly met his demise because of something that had been put in his way, namely a large log and an even more formidable roadblock, a giant boulder.

Before you jump to conspiratorial conclusions, consider that it was not uncommon for trees to fall across railroad tracks in the thick forest of the Coast Range foothills, nor was it uncommon for boulders to roll onto the tracks, loosened by the April showers. Still, it's less common for both events to occur in the same spot, and rarer still for both to happen within minutes of each other, mere moments after the regularly scheduled train had passed the spot with no sign of trouble. That the events happened mere moments before Ben Holladay was scheduled to pass while inspecting the railroad after his hostile takeover from Joseph Gaston surely is coincidental, as is their occurrence on the blind side of a sharp curve. Fortunately for Holladay, a scout sent ahead of his train with a handcar saw the obstruction and was able to have the tycoon's train held in Gaston.

The editors of *The Oregonian*, however, apparently didn't appreciate the odd alignment of events leading up to this near catastrophe. "A Most Dastardly Attempt" was the breathless headline for their April 8 editorial. In their story they point out that one train passed the spot unscathed less than 30 minutes before Holladay's train was due; the railroad tycoon's demise thwarted only by an alert track watcher.

The editorial was written as if to suggest that someone might have wanted to kill Ben Holladay, a man whose only crime was wanting to destroy others, such as Joseph Gaston, who staked his life's dream on a whistlestop near a sharp curve on a failing railroad line. The fact that his bitter rival nearly perished on that sharp curve surely is coincidental.

Rainy Gaston's History has Never Been Dry

The quiet, lush green hills around Gaston long have been a magnet for clean-living religious folk. Cherry Grove and Laurelwood both were built by groups that strictly banned alcohol. Joseph Gaston as well hated the demon rum and called for its prohibition. Even today the Adventists and their successors, the Anandans, the new owners of the Laurelwood Academy, carry on that dry tradition.

Yet somehow those lush, green hills always have attracted people with very different motivations. During Prohibition, which Joe Gaston didn't live to see, hot-rodding moonshiners came to Gaston. In the 1980s and '90s Cherry Grove became known as much for its meth labs as for its rich and amazing history and scenery. Throughout the area there are rickety old barns and sheds with grow lights that aren't there to nurture tomato starts.

The fact that all this sounds a little like Appalachia is not a coincidence. The hills west of Gaston bear many similarities to the Appalachians, home to the infamous moonshiners of the 1920s and early '30s. Prohibition Era Appalachia's remote and rugged green hills were ideal for hiding stills. The sparse, close-knit population made it easy to spot revenuers amidst the familiar faces, and it was a good bet that the local boys could outrun those revenuers on the twisting, remote roads even if the Feds did get wind of their enterprise. Those good old boys got so good at driving that they formed the foundation of today's NASCAR racing circuit. The hills around Gaston were just as good at hiding moonshiners and even hid their own famous race-car driver, but we're getting ahead of ourselves.

This is not how the founders of Gaston, Laurelwood and Cherry Grove envisioned things. Each hoped to establish western Washington County as a beacon for abstinence. August Lovegren put a clause in the deeds to the Cherry Grove houses he sold stating that title would revert back to him if alcohol was found in the home. Even a century later there were hints that abstinence had succeeded, culminating in 1960 when the Dallas Cowboys selected nearby Forest Grove for their training camp because of the area's tradition of dryness, or at least for its illusion of dryness.

In his 1912 *Portland, Oregon, Its History and Builders*, Joseph Gaston addressed the importance of the hops and beer industries to rural Oregon with a certain amount of disdain. "History would be of little account," he wrote, "if it preserved no record of the frivolities, vices and profligacy of mankind." While he acknowledges that Portland breweries annually produced "about a barrel of beer to every man, woman and child in this city," he assures us that much of that actually was destined to "Siberia, China, Japan and the Philippine Islands."

Apparently he thought none of that production was finding its way to Gaston, because in that same year Joseph Gaston told residents of the town that bears his name that no other community "has more faithfully or consistently maintained and taught by honest living and example … the

69

virtues of industry, sobriety, education, morality and religion than this one."

At the time he made this eloquent tribute Joseph Gaston had no way of knowing that the town's doctor and pharmacist, J.A. Baker, would be arrested a few months later for selling "a four-horse load" of whiskey in his "dry" town. He certainly couldn't have known that the "dry" residents of Gaston would elect Baker mayor a few years later, but he might have known that Baker already had been arrested before on the same charge. Worse yet: Poor Joe Gaston died a year after making this speech and four years before Oregon implemented a statewide ban on alcohol in 1916. Had he lived just a few years longer, he would have seen Prohibition become a reality, and he would have seen some of the wildest times in the history of Gaston and its environs.

Tales of Prohibition chicanery have passed through generations with little documentation beyond the fading memories of those who viewed the events as wide-eyed children. Marion Matteson's 92-year-old eyes are no longer wide, but they still are full of life as he recalls growing up in Scoggins Valley in the 1920s and '30s. "We didn't make whiskey and they didn't milk cows; we minded our own business and got along fine," Marion says of the bootleggers, who would come down from the hills to help him bale hay as a youngster on his family's dairy farm.

Young Marion would watch in wonderment after sunset when cars would turn onto the road up Tanner Creek and stop at a certain point. A Morse-code like series of flashes from the headlights would bring an old panel truck rattling down the rutted road with bottles and barrels of

70

whiskey for a thirsty population in the flat lands. This went on for several years, "until some do-gooder called the sheriff," Marion recalls. There was a raid, but the bootleggers "just packed up their pipes and moved down across from the new Stimson Mill."

The new site was much closer to civilization, but offered two distinct advantages: A ready clientele for the illicit spirits and a cover for the distilling process. "On one side of the road you had smoke and steam rising from the mill," Marion recalls, pausing and chuckling, "and then on the other side of the road you had the smoke and steam rising from the still."

Then another do-gooder prompted another raid by the sheriff, Marion recalls, and the bootleggers sought more isolation out west, past the town of Banks. They didn't last long after they left the friendly confines of the Gaston area, however. "Pretty soon," Marion recalls, "The Feds came calling, and the Feds don't give you three days notice before a raid. I don't know what those fellas did for honest employment after that ..."

Marion Matteson's eyes light up again when asked if other forms of chicanery existed in Gaston back in the Roaring '20s. "Oh, yeah," he says, before glancing at the women in his small audience. Always chivalrous, Marion slaps his knee, smiles broadly and just repeats "Oh, yeah ..."

Prohibition barely put a crimp in the lifestyle of Gaston residents; they had been officially dry for a long time and were far too rural to worry needlessly about the prying eyes of law enforcement. Portlanders, on the other hand, were hit harder. The closure of Portland taverns was not welcome news to many people accustomed to the city's nightlife, including a man named Fred Dundee.

Dundee came from one of Oregon's foremost families, including his great-grandfather, Clinton Kelly, one of the state's founders. He married into even more wealth, wedding Esther, the daughter of Henry Brooks, another pioneer. Fred and Esther settled in Portland, where Fred started dabbling in the nascent automobile industry. His car of choice was the White Steamer, an obscure name among the dozens of automakers of the time. He and his uncle opened a White garage on Burnside Street in Portland and the flamboyant Fred soon grabbed the attention of the White Motor Company executives. With the same free spirit of the men who created NASCAR, Fred Dundee loved fast cars and in 1906 White chose him to race its steamers across the West to win publicity for the company. For the next few years he parlayed his risk-taking and outstanding mechanic's skills, racing a Steamer nicknamed "Whistling Billy" and making a name for himself on the track. News concerning Whistling Billy wasn't always good, such as the time in 1909 when it crashed into the crowd at a race in Texas and killed four people, but the car and its driver were much feared in racing circles and generated a steady flow of publicity for Dundee and White.

The news was better for Dundee later in 1909 when President-elect William Howard Taft wanted to show off America's booming auto industry and became the first President to have an official White House car. He chose a White Steamer. Sales of the car took off and Fred Dundee became a very wealthy man. Dundee was a star in the rough-

and-tumble business of cars, famous for entertaining potential clients and partners in royal fashion, showering them with cigars and liquor. When Prohibition came along it put a royal crimp in his style.

In 1921, Dundee found an ideal spot to entertain his business and racing associates in the style to which they had become accustomed, yet just far enough away from the prying eyes of the Portland Police. Just outside Gaston, at the crest of the hills separating Patton and Scoggins valleys, Dundee built a grand lodge, accessible only via a steep, twisty, bumpy dead-end dirt road. Old racer Fred Dundee had no trouble handling the road, but the remote location guaranteed there would be few prying eyes at his 168-acre sylvan retreat. The business of entertaining began anew.

Details are sketchy of exactly what went on up at what Dundee called Dee-Brook Farm and others called the Dundee Lodge. Whatever you call it, it opened in the midst of the Prohibition Era or, as others called it, "the Roaring Twenties." As the Seventh-day Adventist enclave of Laurelwood retreated on Friday evenings for Sabbath observations, Dundee Lodge roared to life. By all accounts, few activities were prohibited among the partygoers. Tales abound of long nights of liquor, gambling and women, sometimes capped off by shooting elk from the wooden decks in the early dawn.

By 1933 Prohibition was dead, victim of the only time America ever repealed a Constitutional amendment. The White Steamer was dead, too, the victim of the internal combustion engine. But 1933 didn't mark the end of Dundee's Portland businesses, which continued to thrive as the White Motor Company transitioned into tractors and trucks, including a partnership with Consolidated Freightways to create the Freightliner brand. When Fred Dundee wasn't partying, he was helping to build Portland into a center of industry. It was a city many of today's residents might not recognize, with not only a Freightliner truck factory but its own Ford assembly plant.

But 1933 didn't mark the end of Gaston's reputation for booze-fueled escapades, either. Not by a long shot, not in a town inhabited by hard-driving, hard-drinking loggers. Perhaps the most notorious joint was the aptly named Shadyside, about a mile down Scoggins Valley Road from the Stimson Mill. Marge O'Rear, too young back in the 1930s to visit the Shadyside herself, recalled 70 years later that "We all heard stories about what went on there. Oh, we heard stories."

Someone who did witness those days at the Shadyside, Ralph Raines, talked about the Shadyside with Lloyd Carl Meyer in 1978 for the Washington County Historical Society's *Land of Tuality*. "Through the '30s and '20s this country here was not quite so civilized as it is now. … You might say that we're past those wild days and in a more civilized era. Really it's better. At my age I don't think I could stand what used to be …"

What used to be, Raines told Meyer, were Saturday nights when a young Raines and his buddies "would get together and speculate where we are going to have the biggest donnybrook tonight." The answer usually was at the Shadyside. "Usually it was just all whiskey fights," he said, recalling one Saturday night in particular. It seems that to control the flow of rowdy patrons into their establishment, the owners nailed shut the side door. Ralph Raines picks up the story: "The loggers all got in a fight one night and they picked up one guy and threw him right through the door! He went right through the door and went right over the bank and right into the creek."

The Shadyside is gone now, too. Winters in Gaston once were much harsher than they are now, and as Raines explained in 1978: "It has now fell down with the snow about 10, 12 years ago, something like that."

The Dundee Lodge has not fallen down, although it has changed dramatically. In 1941, Fred Dundee retired after helping build White Motor Co. and Freightliner and moved to his beloved retreat until his death in 1951. After his death, the lodge languished before coming back to life in the 1970s as the Cherry Grove Center, a retreat with a purpose very different from Dundee's use of the land: promoting wellness and healthy lifestyles. The center closed in 1983 and two years later the Dundee Lodge was placed on the National Register of Historic Places. Soon the once-notorious lodge faded into obscurity and now is a private residence.

Gaston, too, sometimes seems destined for obscurity, although a new industry is breathing life into the town. That industry is, perhaps not surprisingly, alcohol. Smack in the middle between Forest Grove's sake brewery and Carlton's cluster of top-notch wineries, Gaston increasingly is surrounded by rich vineyards. Some of the newest creep up the south side of a hill in Patton Valley, stretching ever closer to the Dundee Lodge.

Business leaders again are bringing clients to Gaston for drinks and entertainment, but usually in the back of a rented limo, not in White Steamers and Model Ts. The parties are sedate and most certainly do not include prostitution or gambling or donnybrooks.

As far as we know.

Dreams of Cheese
Go Up in Smoke

On a hot late summer afternoon in 1993, dense black smoke enveloped Gaston from a spectacular blaze that came to be known as the Cheese Factory Fire.

The building that burned to the ground along Highway 47 on the northern edge of town was not, in fact, a cheese factory that August 27. It recently had been converted to a private residence after decades as the town's school bus barn. But many Augusts before a cutting torch ignited one of Gaston's worst fires ever, the building had indeed been a cheese factory, one that housed the town's dream of becoming Oregon's dairy capital.

Hopes for a Gaston cheese dynasty were so high that the local dairy farmers lured Peter McIntosh, father of Oregon's cheese industry, away from the Tillamook creamery he had led for years. To this day Tillamook's world-famous cheddar is made from McIntosh's recipe. But dreams of cheddar glory were buried in Gaston along with McIntosh when he died in 1940.

The dream was born 20 years earlier. After a decade of battling out-of-state corporate dairy interests, in 1921 the Oregon Dairymen's League built a cheese factory in Gaston in an attempt to better control the price paid to dairy farmers. One of several plants the League built in the state, Gaston's factory got off to a rocky beginning, with local dairy farmers hurling accusations of neglect and mismanagement at the state organization. Within a year, Gaston farmers scraped together the $18,000 necessary to buy the plant and put it into local control.

The cheese factory changed hands several more times but managed to stay afloat, even surviving the Great Depression. When the world-renowned McIntosh decided to make Gaston home in the 1930s, the prospect of becoming the Northwest's pre-eminent dairy town seemed within reach. Then McIntosh died, and towns such as Tillamook and Bandon battled it out for that crown. The flooding of Scoggins Valley for Henry Hagg Lake in the 1970s destroyed nearly all of the few local dairies that clung to survival.

The Cheese Factory became a bus barn before going up in smoke that day in 1993. No sign of it remains. Peter Duncan McIntosh, one of the greatest cheesemakers in American history, lies buried in Gaston's Hill Cemetery, just east of town. From his gravesite one can see for miles. There's not a dairy farm in sight.

Hunters, Dinosaurs and Too Damn Many Deer

Some Gaston-area hunters dream of autumn days spent in the shade of a tree, waiting for a herd of deer or elk to wander into their sights.

The more ambitious don't sit and wait for their prey to meander by. They track elk through the wilderness, even after the weather turns cold and wet. Others track ducks along the Tualatin River. They won't let weather stop them, not after waiting all summer for hunting season to open.

Of course there's another prey to be had in the Gaston area during the spring and summer when hunting is banned. You can fish from shore at Hagg Lake or, if you prefer, from a boat in the middle of the manmade reservoir.

No matter the season, Gaston is a paradise for hunting and fishing, and always has been. The Atfalati people of the Kalapuya made the area the center of their world because of Wapato Lake, which drew deer and elk from the hills during the parched summers and waterfowl the year round. They almost got to keep their hunting grounds because the earliest settlers wanted nothing to do with Wapato Lake, which they saw as a breeding ground for nothing but disease. Instead, the lucky early settlers gobbled up the land in the rich Willamette and Rogue valleys, pushing the Indians to the fringes of the Coast Range, to places such as Wapato Lake.

When all the prime Willamette Valley land was claimed, however, the second wave of settlers had to settle for the areas the Atfalatis still clung to. So the settlers pushed the natives out of those areas, too, and set their sights on draining what they saw as a disease-breeding nuisance, Wapato Lake. There's no record of any of those settlers appreciating the irony in all this; by the time they decided they wanted Wapato Lake they faced little resistance from the Atfalatis, who had been decimated by disease, although not the kind bred in Wapato Lake but rather by the kind transmitted by the white settlers.

Draining the lake proved to be a lot harder than the early settlers expected, and they fought mostly a losing effort for the first 50 years or so. But along the way many people decided the lake's existence in their back yard wasn't so bad after all, especially those years when it came back to life only in the winter, when the mosquitoes weren't so bad. They learned that there was a lot of money to be made from charging trainloads of hunters from Portland to shoot ducks from the railroad tracks. They didn't even mind the winters when the lake froze over. Not at all, in fact, because the ice brought people out for skating and pushed the waterfowl into small corners of the lake that didn't freeze, making them even easier to shoot.

The settlers decided that being pushed up against the rocky walls of the Coast Range had other advantages as well. So what if the soil wasn't quite up to par for raising corn? It was perfect for perhaps an even more lucrative crop: trees. The lucky souls who got the lush Willamette Valley farmland cut down most of their trees, and the Patton and

Scoggins valleys stretched out into the Coast Range forests like super highways, making Gaston the gateway to riches. The Gaston settlers capitalized on this turn of events and then realized yet another advantage to being pushed into the corner they found themselves in: The same early settlers who had pushed them to the fringes had pushed most of the wildlife here as well.

The area always had abundant wildlife to hunt in the hills, but by the dawn of the 20th Century there was no need for hunters to go tracking prey in the woods, not when the prey was coming to the hunters' front yards. "Gaston a Paradise for Bear Hunters," blared a headline in the August 11, 1906, *Oregonian*. The story concerned one W.B. Glafke, a Portland purveyor of bear meat, and Scoggins Valley pioneer Henry Scott, who, the subhead explained, had just "Kill(ed) Two Big Bruins and at Last Accounts Was Chasing a Third Out of His Garden." Bear hunting wasn't just for experienced mountain men like Henry Scott, either, as a headline in *The Oregonian* three years later pointed out: "Scoggins Valley Lads Kill Brute With Tiny Rifles." Times were good for bear hunters in Gaston.

The good times didn't last, however. Although Gaston and Cherry Grove area residents still occasionally bag a bear today, early hunters cut deeply into their numbers and the supply of new bears forced out of the Willamette Valley dried up. At first this turn of events seemed like a blessing to Gaston hunters, not to mention farmers who didn't like the bears killing their livestock. Hunters had killed the bears, and cougars, as much to eliminate competition for deer and elk as for their hides and meat.

Now that the big predators were under control, hunters could kick back and wait for herds to come down to graze and to drink from the river. The established deer trails were well-known, so a little patience often was rewarded, especially as the herds grew. Bears wandering through one's garden became rare.

Unfortunately for the area's farmers, however, there are worse things than having bears in your garden, and high on that list is having a herd of hungry deer in your crops. The problem became particularly acute at the headwaters of the Tualatin, where deer congregated both from the hills and from the valleys and where farmers struggled to raise crops under already tough conditions. By the 1950s, cries of "too many deer!" were common in and around Cherry Grove.

"Too Many Deer" also was the headline in the April 3, 1955, *Oregonian*, on an editorial about angry Cherry Grove farmers who had asked the state for permission to kill deer outside of hunting season and, when their request was denied, had organized a springtime slaughter of the animals. To no one's surprise, the reliably conservative newspaper's editors had sided with the hunters. Much to the editors' surprise, however, most of the newspaper's readers seemed to be squarely at odds with that position.

"The wholesale slaughter of deer by embittered farmers at Cherry Grove has raised public indignation to a pitch not often reached in a discussion of the conduct of a governmental agency," the editorial began. "It is significant that a study of the torrent of letters received by this newspaper shows that more people are angry at the game department for failing to prevent the shooting, or moving to punish it afterward, than at those who pulled the triggers. ... few writers display any real understanding of the problems facing upland farmers and the game department as a result of today's expanded deer population."

We'll have to take the editors at their word that those who objected to the slaughter were a pack of ignorant do-gooders, because the only letter they chose to run on the subject was from someone taking their side of the argument. The letter writer spelled out the reason the deer population had grown in Cherry Grove. It had, he explained, nothing to do with destruction of deer habitat in the valleys or with reduction in the number of natural predators. Instead, he explained, the overpopulation was the result of the Tillamook Burn, which had allowed blackberries and other shrubs favored by deer to gain a temporary foothold while the forests regenerated. When the trees did grow back they pushed out the blackberries and with them the deer, which moved down the hill to Cherry Grove in search of food. The whole crisis was merely a temporary blip, the letter writer assured us, and could be corrected with a couple years of expanded hunting.

So it was that in April 1955, Gaston found itself at Ground Zero in this epic battle, one that rages on today. This particular Sunday the issue dominated the editorial page of the state's largest media empire. Consistent with its First Amendment right, *The Oregonian* advocated only one side of the story that day, although in their flippant dismissal of alternative straw-man arguments, the paper's editors inadvertently poked holes in their own arguments.

For example, the editorial points out that in places such as Cherry Grove, farmers complain during the spring and summer that there are too many deer, and the editors strongly agree with those farmers, hence the headline "Too Many Deer." But after the first paragraph or two, the editorial turns to the lament of hunters that the deer population is too small, and the editors spend most of their time demanding the state ensure an almost endless "harvest" of deer to hunt. Exactly how the "wholesale slaughter" the editors endorsed a few paragraphs earlier contributed to meeting the overriding goal of more deer was left to the reader's imagination.

The authors of the editorial do not address this inherent incongruity in their argument, but do somewhat condescendingly suggest that the simple folk of Cherry Grove were guilty of some sort of hypocrisy in the matter, reminding us that the farmers of summer and the hunters of fall tend to be the same people. To complicate matters, hunters or farmers are tiny minorities in Oregon; according to state records, about 5 percent of Oregonians hunt, with the percentage of real farmers not much higher. In Portland, Salem and Eugene, the state's centers of power and influence, the percentage of each drops perilously close to zero.

But to these big-city editorialists, the issue wasn't so much protecting the interests of native Gastonians as it was protecting "the great economic benefits from the annual invasion of the forests by the army of free-spending hunters." In the end, the goal was to ensure trophies to mount on the walls of "free-spending" city folk, not to ensure the well-being of Gaston's farmers/hunters. More deer would lure more out-of-state hunters, and the problem, the editorialists assured us, would magically take care of itself. But we had to ensure a vast supply of deer because those free-spenders, the editors warned, would just stop hunting if the "sport" became too difficult. The editors tied themselves in twisted knots of logic, but their ultimate point was that bureaucrats can, and must, regulate nature for the benefit of humans.

Not enough deer? Hunt more bears and cougars. Too many deer after killing the predators? Hunt more deer. What happens if after all those years of hunting there aren't enough deer left to guarantee a trophy on every wall? Apparently the answer is to hunt more deer. With such easy answers, some readers might be left wondering why we need any regulation at all.

After all, somehow for millions of years wildlife population issues had resolved themselves without human intervention. Imagine how the editorial pages of 35 million years ago might have covered the hunting situation in and around Gaston. Visiting free-spending hunters back then would not have had the luxury of hiding in the bushes of Patton or Scoggins valley in camouflage, waiting for herds of elk to pass.

Instead, they would have needed boats, and they would have needed boats much sturdier than the ones used to shoot ducks in Wapato Lake or to fish in Hagg Lake. Scientists tell us they would have needed crafts more suitable for salmon fishing off the Coast, because the region's valleys once were filled by an enormous inland sea.

The hardiest of hunters would not have been content with a salmon, either; their prize would have been a shark.

We know there were sharks in the area not because of hunters in big boats, however, but rather because of fossil hunters scouring the dry sea bed back in the 1950s, long after volcanic eruptions and landslides drained the ancient sea. So hunters are out of luck if they want to bag a shark in Gaston today. Ironically, even fossil hunters might be out of luck today. The dry sea bed those fossils were found in was in Scoggins Valley, most of which is now buried under man-made Hagg Lake, where once again people go fishing, but with a much more humble catch in mind.

Even a shark, however, would not have yielded the trophy a hunter might have found a mere 15,000 years ago in Gaston. Imagine, if you will, the mount from an animal 20 feet long and weighing three or four tons.

The remains of just such an animal were found in the 1960s and '70s, downstream from Gaston near the city of Tualatin. For many years the fossil bones were believed to have come from a mastodon, conjuring images of elephants traipsing through the valley. Over time, however, researchers re-evaluated the remains and decided the animal was more like a bear with huge paws. Today's hunters might shudder at the thought of how many deer a beast like that might gobble up before hunting season opened.

But in 2010, experts from Portland State University told the *Valley Times* of Beaverton that this creature wasn't a bear at all, but rather an incredibly large sloth. So if these sloths were like those that roam the Earth today, they would have eaten leaves and twigs and wouldn't have been any competition at all for deer hunters. Not only that, if the creature shared today's sloths' notoriously slow gait, hunters wouldn't need hounds to track it. On the other hand, if it lived in trees like its present-day cousins, hunters would have had to be very careful about resting in the shade of an old oak tree, especially after the sloth's dinner time.

The truth is that we don't know if there were too many or too few sharks and sloths back then, because only modern humans are audacious enough to make such determinations. A hunter 15,000 years ago would have to kill only one giant sloth to feed an entire village, but if every person in the village wanted a sloth head hanging on his wall, the beasts probably would have seemed scarce. And when the hunter went back to farming in the spring, even one six-ton behemoth trampling his rutabagas would have seemed like far too many. Yet all this is, of course, a moot point. Nature settled the shark and sloth population issues long ago without seeking the opinion of hunters, environmentalists or editorial writers.

Even a mere 100 years before the Cherry Grove deer slaughter, wildlife population issues didn't concern humans in Gaston so very much. The area's indigenous people didn't make such quantitative analyses. As long as there were just enough deer and elk to feed their families they were filled with nothing but gratitude. They didn't concern themselves with whether there were enough to lure free-spending hunters from outside the area. Perhaps the Kalapuya knew that their lives and culture would be destroyed if and when those folks ever arrived.

All of which brings us back to present-day Gaston. Most of today's local hunters are not of the free-spending variety. In fact for many, raising enough cash to buy a license and gun is a stretch, and taking time off work to hunt often means they don't get paid. Just as in 1955, nearly every one of today's local hunters has an opinion about the supply of wildlife, and just as then those opinions tend to shift depending on whether they're worried about their tomato crop or worried that their tag will expire after days in the cold rain, days spent without seeing a deer.

In the end, just like the Indians, most of these local hunters are more than happy as long as they find just one deer, because that could mean the difference between feeding their families or going on food stamps. Of course some of the local hunters don't need the meat for survival, and many of them selflessly share their "trophy" with their not-so-fortunate friends.

These hunters are not the ones most city dwellers read about, however. They are more likely to read about high-paid corporate mouthpieces prattling on about the right of hunters to own high-powered assault rifles, rifles most of Gaston's hunters could never afford, choosing instead to get along with the old rifle they inherited from their father after he died young, after a rugged life as a logger.

In Oregon, most of the 5 percent of the population that hunts feels embattled, but the subsistence hunters of Gaston have a right to feel both embattled *and* ignored. Hunting is portrayed today much as it was in 1955, as a sport to be enjoyed by the leisure class. Yet what about the forgotten hunters of Gaston when the leisure class sportsmen kill all the deer they want? That is precisely when government regulation becomes essential, the editorial writers tell us:

"The meat hunter who is interested only in a winter's supply of venison may find the pickings slim, but the (game) department need feel no great pangs about sending him back to the butcher shop counter."

Let him eat filet mignon …

Too Damn Many Buffalo

There is no more iconic symbol of the American West than the bison.

When William Cody established his Wild West Show, for example, he didn't call himself "Water Rights Willie" or "Donation Land Claim Cody." He chose "Buffalo Bill." Likewise, I couldn't claim that Gaston is the perfect metaphor for the American West without including something about buffalo.

Unfortunately Gaston's early history doesn't yield many buffalo stories. Although there are reports of buffalo bones having been found across the state in far eastern Oregon, no herds ever made it to Gaston, at least not of their own accord. But that doesn't mean Gaston doesn't have a great buffalo story, because it does, and it's one that tells the story of the buffalo as well as any town in the Great Plains could.

Of course some of Gaston's early settlers probably hunted buffalo on their way out here across the Oregon Trail. The government actively encouraged such hunting, because there were just too damn many buffalo in the Plains competing with the settlers, eating their cattle's grass, trampling their crops and derailing their trains.

But even by the time many of Gaston's immigrants arrived there were signs that the herds were being hunted to extinction. "Buffalo Bill" Cody was one of the first to ask Congress for protections to prevent the extinction, but it turns out extinction is exactly what many in the government wanted, not because they hated buffalo, but rather because they hated Indians. The Army led the effort, and author Brian Bergman explains the rationale in *Bison: Back From the Brink of Extinction*. Gen. Philip Sheridan told Congress in 1875 that buffalo hunters had done more than his own Army had to resolve "the vexed Indian question," by depriving the Indians of their main food source, buffalo. And by Sheridan's estimation – one he shared with his commander-in-chief, President Ulysses Grant – Congress shouldn't be worried about extinction because there *still* were too damn many buffalo. "For the sake of a lasting peace," Sheridan urged Congress, "let them kill, skin and sell until the buffaloes are exterminated."

So, what does any of this have to do with Gaston? Well, Phil Sheridan gets us close, as close as nearby Yamhill. Sheridan commanded Fort Yamhill, established to keep the Kalapuya from trying to sneak back through the Wapato Gap to their old stomping grounds around Wapato Lake. Sheridan loved the area so much he bought land there and retired to Oregon when his Army career ended. The town of Sheridan, home of the Grand Ronde tribe's lavish Spirit Mountain Casino, is named for the man who wanted to starve Indians by slaughtering the buffalo.

Now to get back to those Gaston settlers. Thanks to Phil Sheridan and Fort Yamhill they didn't have to worry about Indians. And, unlike their brethren in the Plains, they never had buffalo to compete with their cattle, so the area developed a thriving dairy industry.

Raising cows in the buffalo-free fields of Gaston, enough milk was produced that in time the town had its own cheese factory, one that rivaled any on the West Coast. Until, long story short, corporate interests crushed the independent Gaston farmers and the dairy industry is all but gone today.

Now that the fields were mostly cow-free, Gaston farmers needed a new cash crop. For some it was wine, for others ornamental nursery stock. But for some, the answer was to fill their fields with – wait for it – buffalo. Buffalo meat has become a highly sought-after gourmet item, and Gaston farmers caught the trend early.

Still, Gaston's buffalo story can be told best from the perspective of the area's pioneers. Not that most of them had much experience with buffalo, because they didn't; it's likely that some never even saw one. But many of them are buried in Hill Cemetery, just east of town. Hill Cemetery is named after pioneer Almoran Hill, but by coincidence it also sits on a hill, one that overlooks a vast agricultural valley. When you stand in the cemetery today you won't see any dairy cows in the fields. You will see acres of ornamental nursery stock and if you peer off into the distance you can see some of Gaston's lush vineyards. But mostly what you'll notice is that you're surrounded by a herd of buffalo.

People in towns in places like Montana and South Dakota and Wyoming will tell you that they have better buffalo stories than Gaston, stories of the old days when they had millions of buffalo running free, etc. But really, they're probably just jealous. Nationally, nearly 35,000 domesticated buffaloes like the ones around Hill Cemetery are sent to the butcher to be sold in grocery stores. That's

35,000 every year. Yet by most estimates there are only about 15,000 wild bison left in the country, and that's total.

So just try to make a story out of that, Cody, Wyoming. Your namesake, "Buffalo Bill," isn't around anymore to promote your interests, but we have Safeway to promote ours.

1850:
Not Just Another Year

1850 is the year in which the West was won, or lost, depending on your perspective.

1850 was an especially interesting year for Gaston, except of course Gaston didn't exist in 1850. Gaston exists *because* of 1850.

Because of a series of seemingly unrelated events in 1850, a typical day for a typical modern Gaston resident might look something like this: A stop at the Gaston City Hall to pay a water bill before driving 50 miles to the lavish Spirit Mountain Casino after a day spent working at the Stimson Mill on Scoggins Valley Road or relaxing at a Hagg Lake beach a mile from the mill.

If not for those events in 1850, that typical day might look like this: A stop at the Matteson City Hall to pay a water bill before walking a few steps across the road to the lavish Wapato Lake Casino after a day working at the Stimson Mill on Patton Valley Road or relaxing at a Lovegren Lake beach a mile from the mill.

Confused? Don't be. The answer is as simple as a coin flip. Well, sometimes it's not that simple, and instead entails a broken federal treaty from before Oregon was a state. OK, and other times it involves a convoluted law intended to rid Louisiana of malaria but which instead ended up creating cornfields in Iowa and onion fields in the Tuality Plains of Oregon. And if you really want to get technical, if not for the events of 1850 we might never have heard the names Gaston, Matteson, Lovegren, Patton, Hagg, Scoggin ...

Yet all of us in these parts have heard those names because, well, 1850 was a very interesting year. It's the year this little piece of the West was won, or lost, again depending on your perspective.

Let's return for a moment to 1850, an important year in the white man's first major incursion into the Willamette, Tualatin and Rogue valleys of the Oregon Territory. Native Americans were willing to share the rich farmlands and the bountiful hunting and fishing grounds with the settlers, but 1850 was the year the settlers decided they really just wanted it all for themselves.

To the south, the Rogue Valley War was raging between settlers and Indians, but in the northern valleys around what is now Gaston both sides were working toward a more peaceful solution. Forced from most of their land at gunpoint, the Kalapuya tribes along the Tualatin and Yamhill rivers offered to give up nearly all of their ancestral land in exchange for some measure of peace.

The battered Kalapuya had been backed into a corner not so much as a result of violence but from the horrifying illnesses the settlers spread, illnesses to which they had no immunity. By many estimates, the tribe had lost all but about 400 of its members by 1850. With little strength left to fight, they asked only for a corner of the Tualatin Valley the settlers didn't really want anyway, the area around mosquito-ridden Wapato Lake. The Indians loved the lake for the birds and wildlife it attracted and for the bountiful wapato root vegetables that flourished in the black peat of its shores. The white settlers dismissed the lake as a disease-laden swamp with little or no value, so a treaty was worked out for the Kalapuya people. They would get the lake in exchange for surrendering any claim to the rich farm and timberlands that surrounded it, and for protection from the federal government against attacks from settlers who weren't willing to settle for anything less than annihilation of an entire race of people.

All things considered, given their decimated ranks and the violence raging elsewhere, the Kalapuya did about as well as could be expected in the treaty. With the exception of a few hotheads, most of the settlers who had made the rugged journey over the Oregon Trail had come to realize that the treasure of Oregon was bountiful enough that they could afford to leave the indigenous people a few crumbs. Or swamps.

When the treaty was signed, the Kalapuya certainly didn't envision a glitzy casino at Wapato Lake like the one that sprang up about 50 miles south and 140 years later on tribal land near Sheridan. Instead, in 1851 they hunkered down with nothing but a treaty agreement and raw survival on their minds, which they might have achieved if not for some conniving back in Washington, D.C.

The Oregon settlers who signed the treaty actually had betrayed the charge they had been given by Congress, which had ordered the complete removal of all indigenous people from the valleys, to be exiled to points east of the Cascades to terrain, a climate and an ecosystem that would have been entirely foreign to them. But such a magnanimous spirit would never do for bureaucrats and businessmen intoxicated by a sense of Manifest Destiny back in the nation's Capital. With the Indian Wars raging elsewhere in the West, in February of 1851 Congress yanked the rug out from under the Treaty Commissions such as the one in Oregon. Communications being what they were back then, word of that action didn't reach Oregon for months, after the treaty had been signed, sealed and delivered. But Congress considered it null and void.

The Kalapuya had lost another battle, but continued to seek a peaceful solution. Increasingly greedy settlers weren't so accommodating and stepped up harassment of the remaining tribal members. In 1855, another treaty was signed, promising the Kalapuyas a reservation in the Willamette Valley. The treaty just didn't specify exactly where in the Willamette Valley, and soon the Kalapuya were forcibly removed to the Coast Range, where their numbers continued to dwindle until they no longer were officially recognized by the federal government. Finally in the 1980s, the Kalapuya and remnants of other local native people regained federal recognition as the Confederated Tribes of the Grand Ronde, and a grand casino rose near Sheridan, pumping millions of dollars into the local economy. Some of the people headed to the casino from Portland cruise through Gaston on Highway 47, but few stop in the town.

Back in 1850, however, white settlers were not concerned with future casinos. In 1850 they were more concerned with what to do about all this free land they had acquired. How, they asked Congress, shall we divide this bounty? Luckily for the settlers, Congress was an industrious group back then, capable of doing much more than simply negating negotiated treaties, and it quickly passed the Donation Land Claim Act.

In essence, the law granted 320 acres to any white man who arrived in Oregon by 1850 and half that to anyone who arrived by 1854. The law was ahead of its time in one respect: It also granted 320 acres to any white woman, as long as she happened to be married to one of the white guys who got his own 320 acres. It was one of the first acts of Congress granting women (almost) equal land-ownership rights with men. It even magnanimously granted the privilege to Native American men ... as long as only one of their parents was Indian, the other being white. Perhaps only coincidentally, the second treaty with the Kalapuya (the one that exiled them to Sheridan) wasn't signed until the year the Land Grant law expired and white people had claimed all the land they wanted.

Most of the area that would become Gaston was settled by people with those donation land claims, including people with names such as Matteson, Patton, Bridgefarmer, Horner, Gerrish ... A couple have entire valleys named after them, some have familiar streets or roads named for them, and still others things named after them that most residents don't even know are named for just plain folk. For example, Hill Creek, Hill Cemetery and Hill School did not get their names from the hills they occupy or originate from, but rather from adventurous Donation Land Claim beneficiary Almoran Hill. None of the local settlers, however, has an entire town named after him, although one almost did.

The man for whom Gaston is named did not have a donation land grant, but he figured out a way to get an even more-massive gift from the federal government; it turned out that the generous Congress of 1850 had already unknowingly obliged him. Joseph Gaston was a man who knew how to work the system, although sometimes not as well as he thought. True, he won the right-of-way for the Westside rail line from Portland to Corvallis, but that was small consolation for the prize that got finagled out from under him by Ben Holladay: the lucrative Eastside rail line connecting Portland to Salem, Eugene, California ... and the rest of North America ...

Anyway, Gaston fumed for the rest of his life about the underhanded dealings that cost him the Eastside line, but still a federal railroad right-of-way is pretty good stuff, and Gaston's came right through the Wapato Gap. But he didn't build his town in the Gap. He had his eye on the same prize the Indians coveted, Wapato Lake, but for very different reasons. Enter the third event of 1850 that would forever alter the town's history, although this event originally had nothing to do with Oregon and wouldn't be felt here until almost 20 years later.

Remember, back in 1850 the land around Wapato Lake was so undesirable to the white settlers that they were willing to give it to the Indians. The Indians called it a "lake," the settlers a "swamp." In 1850 no one wanted a swamp. In fact, Congress wanted every swamp eliminated and offered to give anything considered a swamp to anyone willing to drain it. The Swamp Act of 1849 applied only to Louisiana, but once entrepreneurs realized the potential financial bonanza the Swamp Act offered, they lobbied Congress to extend the law. In 1850, Congress decided that "swamp" could apply to wet ground elsewhere.

Congress never really defined what a "swamp" was, except that it was land considered unfit for cultivation. In other words, swampiness was all in the eye of the beholder, and the eye that beheld Wapato Lake in the 1860s belonged to Joseph Gaston, while surveying a route for his railroad. Gaston had missed out on the Donation Land Grant craze of 1850-55, but the Swamp Act was in some ways even better, putting no legal limit to how large an area could be given to an individual or couple. Wapato Lake was much bigger than any land grant, and soon it belonged to Joseph Gaston.

Gaston tried for 15 years to fully drain Wapato Lake with only limited success. In the late 1800s people did not appreciate or understand the necessity of "swamps," what we now call "wetlands," in the ecosystems. Wapato Lake was a crucial element in filtering and controlling runoff in the Tualatin River watershed, and as such it flooded nearly every winter despite Gaston's best efforts. Joseph Gaston was the area's largest landowner, but his land remained useless as a townsite, and he needed a settlement to serve his fledgling railroad. His Swamp Act claim just didn't fit the bill.

The ideal townsite was on the hill just west of Wapato Lake, on the donation land claim of Alveris Matteson. Alveris' great-grandson, Marion, picks up the story from there, as told to George Ing for his book *Wending the Way from Wapato Gap*. Joe Gaston wanted a chunk of Alveris' land, and Alveris was willing to sell him 20 acres ...

100

with the condition that they flip a coin to determine whether the town would be called "Gaston" or "Matteson." City slicker Joe Gaston won the coin flip over country bumpkin Al Matteson.

Joseph Gaston died in California in 1913, just days after the town of Gaston's civic leaders voted to formally incorporate as a city.

The Mattesons, on the other hand, remain active in the area still today, almost 150 years after the coin flip, but without a town to show for their efforts. There is, however, a dirt road that bears their name. It's just south of the city of Gaston.

Finally, the reasons that Hagg Lake and the Stimson Mill are in Scoggins Valley instead of Patton Valley are equally complicated, but based less on happenstance than on hard-nosed business dealings. The planners for both the mill and the lake coveted the Tualatin River as it roared into Patton Valley but had to settle for the comparative trickle of Scoggins, Sain and Tanner creeks in Scoggins Valley instead.

C.W. Stimson had his eye on what was left of August Lovegren's mill site after the Cherry Grove dam disaster, but after negotiations with Lovegren's successors fell apart, he settled for Scoggins Valley instead.

In the 1960s when farmers scanned the hills for a source of irrigation water, their attention was drawn to the Tualatin as well. After years of studies and meetings, they, like Stimson, had to settle for Scoggins Valley instead. Many of those who favored the Patton Valley site blamed a familiar nemesis of farmers in the area: the Indians. The

Patton Valley's rich Native American heritage, they said, is what caused Scoggins Valley's land to be taken and buried under water instead. There's truth to that claim, but there's another familiar theme at play, one that also is common in the development of the American West: money and power. Patton Valley always has had more of each.

So today motorists headed down Highway 47 can take a detour up Scoggins Valley Road to visit Hagg Lake. On the way they'll pass the Stimson Mill. Headed on south, they'll probably sail right on past Patton Valley without even noticing it, slow down (but probably not stop) in Gaston, then pick up speed again only to blow past Matteson Road.

Most will never know how coin flips, dirty business deals, the war against Indians and Louisiana swamps all shaped the landscape they're passing through on their way to the big casino near Sheridan.

They'll never know just what an interesting year 1850 really was.

10-4, This is Gaston's Ghost Cruiser

Gaston has a police car. Sometimes you see it parked in front of City Hall, a reminder for Portlanders headed toward Spirit Mountain Casino to slow the heck down.

If motorists think they see an officer in the police car, however, they're really seeing an apparition, the ghost of police chiefs past. Because while Gaston has a police car, it doesn't have any police officers. Not anymore. Not after a string of misfortunes that included a couple of chiefs going to jail.

The low point came between October 1976, when one chief was convicted of theft and official misconduct, and January 1977, when his successor was arrested and charged with statutory rape and furnishing marijuana to a 14-year-old girl.

But the fact that Gaston no longer has a police department has less to do with misconduct by a couple of individuals than it does with societal changes that have affected small towns across America. Most of the men who held the job were honest and able; Gaston's tax base ultimately simply wasn't able to support them the way they deserved to be.

The city finally gave up in 2003 and contracted with the Washington County Sheriff's Office to provide police services. The move followed a trend in which small Oregon towns decided they no longer could afford the staffing and training necessary to operate their own departments. It also followed the suicide of Gaston's last police chief.

Like every town, Gaston always has had crime. It always has had law enforcement, too, even if it wasn't always deemed adequate back in the town's Wild West days, as in the case of blacksmith David Porter.

By 1904, Porter was in his 60s and married to a woman, described by the press as "comely," nearly 30 years younger. The couple had four children together, but Porter's wife threw him out of the house and divorced him. After the divorce he took up residence in his blacksmith shop, which not by happenstance was directly next door to his former home where his children and ex-wife still lived.

The former Mrs. Porter complained to the town marshal repeatedly about the drunken blacksmith's amorous advances and physical assaults and several times the marshal intervened, but not to Mrs. Porter's satisfaction. An article in *The Oregonian* picks up the story from there: "Several weeks ago …, wearying of the law's inadequate measures, (she) tied him hand and foot. Since then he has been a very meek member of society."

The reporter handled the story as something of a joke, which is apparently how Mrs. Porter thought local law enforcement was handling her complaints. The paper continues: "(O)n Saturday night (Porter) gathered in some Dutch courage and attempted to force an entrance to the home of the woman who once had shared everything with him. He was met at the door … with a dangerous looking gun, which exploded twice in his face."

Porter was uninjured, but the story still made Page 1 of *The Oregonian* for an odd reason. The headline read "Woman Uses A Gun," and the lead began: "Gaston has been shaken and rather amused by a serio-comic shooting affair that occurred there last Saturday night. That the person who handled the gun was a woman had added to the clamor of tongues ..."

The story tells us much about the early 1900s, when domestic abuse was ignored, tolerated, or even laughed at. Mrs. Porter wasn't laughing that night, telling police "I have had enough of him." A few months later, no one was laughing as Porter sat in jail on charges of raping his ex-wife. The story also illustrates one of the problems small towns such as Gaston face with law-enforcement efforts: Small budgets often mean towns are forced to hire young, sometimes less than highly trained police chiefs who are not equipped to deal with complicated or violent crimes.

The police chief charged with theft in 1976 was 24. His successor, charged with statutory rape, was 28. The chief who committed suicide in 2003 was older at 42, but before being hired in Gaston his experience consisted of being a reserve deputy in a rural county.

The Gaston area was rocked by violent and confusing deaths in 1905 and 1908, but then settled into decades of relative peace. When a town council formed in 1913 to establish a city, its first official act was to authorize construction of a jail and to hire a marshal to staff it, but over the years the facility ended up housing more inebriated misfits than incorrigible miscreants. With a very low cost of living, the city could afford enough to pay its police chief a reasonable, albeit modest, family wage, attracting a string of able and honorable men to the position. Many, such as 1950s-era Alvin Chapman, served for years both as police chief and fire chief.

But back in the day that Gaston could afford a top-notch police chief, the town had many assets it lacks today. Back then, Gaston had hotels and stores, including two department stores. It had a prosperous feed mill, sawmill, bank, gas stations and prosperous doctors, lawyers and other services, all of which generated revenue for the city. By the 1960s, however, Gaston and many other small rural towns had lost nearly all of their commercial tax base. In the 1970s inflation sent the cost of living soaring, along with salaries of big-city police officers. Then in the 1980s tax revolts limited the stream of residential tax revenue. Gaston and other rural communities no longer could afford to attract top-quality police chiefs, or at least retain the ones they did happen to land.

All the while, tighter drug laws were sending drug prices spiraling upward and drug users spiraling downward into lives of crime. The crimes necessary to pay for higher drug prices became more complex and sophisticated. Big cities had money to spend on the Drug Wars; towns like Gaston didn't. All this sent many small-town police forces into a death spiral.

Gaston soldiered on, hiring a string of police chiefs. Most were young, about the same age as most of the town's criminal element, but most performed at least adequately, if not well. Others performed not so well.

The mid-1970s were wild times in America. Members of the Baby Boom generation were becoming young adults, which created a huge wave of people in their prime crime years, many of whom experimented with drugs and indulged in all manner of fads and fashions. Police chiefs in their 20s were not necessarily immune from societal peer pressure, especially when they had little supervision and few professional peers to keep an eye on them.

In 1976, one of the hottest fads was the citizens band radio. C.W. McCall had a monster hit with "Convoy," and soon "Smokey and the Bandit" would become one of the signature movies of the decade. Everyone wanted a CB radio, especially young people in rural towns like Gaston, so it really was no surprise that Gaston's 24-year-old police chief would catch a group of young men red-handed with a cache of stolen CBs. It is a disappointment, although again probably not a huge surprise, that the young police chief would choose to keep the stolen CBs for himself instead of returning them to their rightful owners, but that's what Gaston's chief was convicted of doing. He received two 5-year prison terms.

Gaston quickly replaced him with an older chief, one who was all of 28. But less than three months after his predecessor was sentenced, the new chief was in jail himself, accused of falling under the spell of an even more powerful lure for young men: Sex.

By the late 1970s, society took sex crimes more seriously than they did when old blacksmith David Porter was terrorizing his ex-wife. When the charge was that a 28-

year-old man took a 14-year-old girl from her home 150 miles away, gave her marijuana and had sex with her for many months, 1977-vintage police officers and prosecutors took notice. When that 28-year-old is the newly named police chief of Gaston, pretty much everyone took notice.

In fairness, the young police chief was something of a victim of the times in which served. For the first 80 or so years of Gaston's history, having consensual sex with a 14-year-old might well have earned the police chief a visit from the girl's shotgun-toting pappy, but it would not have earned him a trip to the slammer. In fact, 20 years earlier on Halloween Day 1956, a Gaston woman made the top of *The Oregonian*'s front page when she became a grandmother at age 32. Both she and her daughter married when they were 14; the elder woman to a 42-year-old man. Times change, however, and in 1977 having sex with a 14-year-old was enough to put another Gaston police chief behind bars.

By the time the Washington County Jail doors clanged shut behind him in 1977, the Gaston area was wrapping up what by any standard was among its worst 12 months ever. Two police chiefs in jail. Four people, including two little girls, brutally executed. The hottest, driest summer in decades, resulting in crop losses and the area's worst-ever grass fire season. A blaze in the town's diner ...

Gaston's civic leaders could have thrown up their hands right there and turned local law enforcement over to the county, the state, or anyone else willing (or foolish enough) to take it. They didn't. They hired another young police chief, and then another. By the mid-1980s, things had quieted down. Craig Phillips, the chief in 1984, told the local newspaper he could recall only one drug arrest in the past seven years. No Gaston police chief had gone to jail in those seven years, either, so things looked pretty rosy again in Gaston, at least on the surface.

By 1984 Oregon was in the midst of another timber-fueled recession that hit towns such as Gaston particularly hard. Many of its few remaining businesses were closing and there was a very real possibility the town's schools would be gobbled up by Forest Grove, driving another dagger into the town's pride. Chief Phillips' integrity and qualifications never were in question, but his job security nevertheless remained tenuous.

And while Phillips might have been aware of only one drug arrest in the city limits, other police agencies were well aware there was drug activity in the hills and valleys that surrounded the town. Although they rarely knew the exact location, cops knew people were growing pot, and probably lots of it. The near rain-forest conditions, especially just west of town, provided ideal conditions and cover for grow operations. Even more ominously, 1983 marked the start of a scourge that swept through rural America: The easily produced, relatively cheap, extremely addictive methamphetamine, or meth.

The revolving door at the police chief's office continued through the 1990s, but not because the chiefs were being arrested. Now the problem was different: Gaston was hiring bright, young, well-trained chiefs. They were so well-trained, in fact, that bigger agencies were snapping them up, and Gaston's meager coffers didn't hold enough cash to compete with sheriff's departments and state agencies to retain them. Todd Hoodenpyl was such a young man.

Hoodenpyl joined the department as a volunteer reserve officer in June 1993. Less than a year later he was appointed chief and took over a department that he acknowledged was in "very, very poor shape." But soon the 24-year-old chief was earning praise from other agencies for how well he had tackled the tough job, which he told the *Forest Grove News-Times* was "a very good educational experience." It turned out to be such a good education that two years after volunteering as a reserve, Hoodenpyl's time as chief ended when he was hired by the Oregon State Police and assigned to the east side of the state. "For the third time in four years," the *News-Times* reported, "Gaston will have to appoint a new police chief."

By comparison, the town's fire department had been a picture of stability, thanks in large part to one of Todd Hoodenpyl's relatives, Ron Hoodenpyl, who had been fire chief for more than 30 years. Unfortunately for Gaston, Ron had decided to retire in the early '90s and now the fire department was going through its own revolving door process of finding his successor. Disagreements over who should be chief had reached the point that by 1995 the nearly all-volunteer fire department, as well as the rest of the town, was in a state of turmoil that made the police department's issues look tame by comparison. Long-time volunteers slammed down their pagers and resigned at anger-filled board meetings and families that had been friends for years stopped speaking when they found themselves on opposite sides in the debate.

The two departments were dealing with many of the same issues. The 1990s saw the state and federal governments raising the standards for public-safety agencies, and one of the goals was to bring uniformity in rules and practices. That meant that Gaston suddenly had to meet the same standards as Portland, but with a tiny fraction of Portland's tax base. Gaston might have felt alone in its strife in the mid-1990s, but in reality the turmoil was playing out in rural communities across the country.

The fire department had several huge advantages over the police department, however, and its turmoil was relatively short-lived. For one thing, the city of Gaston had realized nearly 30 years earlier that it could not go it alone in the world of firefighting and merged its department with the rural volunteer department that circled the city. With Laurelwood, Cherry Grove, Patton Valley and Scoggins Valley in the fold, the fire district had a much more stable pool of money with which to operate; the town of Gaston, in fact, was little more than 10 percent of the population of the Gaston Fire District.

But the fire department had an even bigger advantage in finding an answer to balancing its need for a city-level chief with the reality of a rural budget. The firefighters were nearly all volunteers, so crews were available 24 hours a day, 365 days a year. The chief could be part-time, allowing the department to hire a semi-retired, highly experienced firefighter from a big department to lead the eager volunteers. The fire chief doesn't have to respond to every call of an illegal bonfire or twisted ankle. Plus, with its bigger tax base, the district had enough money left over to pay one or two other firefighters.

The police department didn't have those luxuries. It had barely enough money for one officer, and not a very well-paid one, either. It's hard to find an experienced officer from a bigger town willing to spend his or her "retirement" responding to every report of a fender-bender or stolen hubcap. Nor is it easy to find an eager 21-year-old with the experience to handle volatile domestic disturbances and felony drug arrests, and even harder to keep him when you do find one. Being police chief in a small town can be a very lonely experience.

People in small towns are predisposed to like firefighters who arrive to help them, especially volunteers they have known for years. It's common for firefighters to arrive at a small fire or medical call and find themselves chatting with the person they're helping about their grandchildren or most recent hunting trip. Police officers, on the other hand, often are not a welcome sight when they pull over a neighbor for speeding or haul another neighbor to jail on a warrant. When firefighters do have an uncomfortable experience, they go back to the station to find comfort and support from their fellow volunteers. When the lone cop gets done with a bad call, he goes back to work alone, cruising the dark streets, knowing the band of teenagers on the street corner might be giving him the finger behind his back. Being a police chief in a small town can be a lonely job indeed.

By the late 1980s meth labs were becoming common in the rural Midwest and South, and they were popping up in Oregon as well. Not surprisingly, the winding, rugged, dead-end roads and dense vegetation of the Patton Valley and surrounding hills were an ideal location for Oregon's fledgling meth cookers. While officers in the surrounding areas were very busy with meth labs and meth-fueled crime, Gaston's Chief Phillips still could report almost no drug problems in town. So it's ironic that in the end it would be a meth arrest outside the city limits that would be the death knell for the Gaston Police Department.

By 2003, Gaston seemingly had shaken its police department curse. There had been some grumbling about the town's current chief, mostly for what some perceived as a lack of experience for the job, but in his years on the job he had put to rest most of those concerns. He was, by all accounts, a capable and likable officer, well respected in the community.

Things began to unravel for him, however, when police in nearby Hillsboro arrested a young woman for possession of meth. It all was pretty routine by now in Oregon, except for what the young woman asked one of the arresting officers. What if, she asked, I could spill the beans on a crooked cop? No cop ever wants to be dragged into an investigation that might bring down a brother officer, but most officers don't like a dirty cop either, so they listened.

The allegedly "dirty cop" in question was Gaston's police chief. The drug suspect laid out a series of allegations to detectives, who launched an investigation. Gaston's chief acknowledged that he had been romantically involved with the woman, but denied any wrongdoing. Still, state and county police kept digging, determined that if he were guilty they would send him to jail as they had his predecessors in the 1970s. They dug, and Gaston's city officials cooperated. Many in the community came to the chief's defense, and almost no one spoke ill of him, with the notable exception of the young woman facing drug charges in Hillsboro.

Detectives gave prosecutors what they had, and everyone agreed there was no criminal complaint to be made against Gaston's chief. The state looked for ethical breaches and came up empty as well. Gaston's city council and attorney met and offered the chief their full support. There would be no repeat of 1976 and '77. Gaston's police chief was clean, and the town was eager for him to stay on.

But this chief left of his own accord, and he left abruptly. No one is sure why, because everyone agreed his only offense was that he had once been attracted to a woman who later was arrested for meth. But something was eating at him, because at about 4:30 p.m. Thursday, September 11, 2003, a motorist saw a car on the side of the road next to a bird sanctuary in nearby Forest Grove with what he thought was a man's body on the ground next to it.

When police arrived they found a privately owned car with the body of a man dressed in civilian clothes lying dead, clutching a handgun. Although the man had gone to great length to not call attention to the fact, officers knew immediately that he was Gaston's current police chief. They didn't know that he would be the town's last.

Gaston's city council members considered their options, and decided to get out of the police business. They contracted with the Washington County Sheriff's Office for protection. Overnight, Gaston went from a poorly paid, poorly staffed, poorly equipped police force to being part of one of Oregon's largest, best-equipped and best-trained law enforcement agencies.

The county stationed a full-time deputy in town. Unlike Gaston's city police, this deputy was not restrained by the city limits, and his investigations led him to meth labs and criminals in the surrounding areas, particularly Cherry Grove, that had managed for decades to fly under law-enforcement radar.

As much as locals welcomed the beefed-up enforcement efforts and liked the resident deputies, some still felt a sense of loss. One rarely sees headlines about new businesses, employers or anything good moving into Gaston. More often the town experiences loss, a slow but steady erosion of its identity and pride.

The family sawmills are gone, as are the signature onion fields. Even the railroad tracks that gave birth to the town in the first place are gone. So too now is the police department, of which only a trace remains, because the town kept its police car.

Sometimes when you drive through town you'll see the police cruiser in front of City Hall, a gray Ford with "Gaston Police" on its doors. It's a ghost cruiser of a sort, haunted by the stories of police chiefs past. It's also a haunting reminder of Gaston's many losses over the years, and what some might see as decay.

Yet in other ways the cruiser is a testament to the town's future. We know that no Gaston cop is going to use it to protect us, but then again we know the cops who will come to our aid have modern marvels Gaston could never afford. We know that while it's a symbol of our slow loss of identity, the ghost police car also is a symbol of our small-town pride and ingenuity, a clever speed trap that costs us nothing, a subtle middle finger raised at urban sophisticates who want to smirk when they see our town ... but instead hit their brakes in a panic.

Those of us who know Gaston aren't afraid of the cruiser when it's parked on Front Street, nor are we afraid of the ghosts that might inhabit it. We just drive on by, never taking a second glance into our rear-view mirrors. Times change, and we change with the times.

Going 5 in a 4 mph Zone

For a few years in the early part of this century, Gaston was well-known for the frequent speed traps along Front Street, where the speed limit is 30 miles per hour. On either side of the city limits, Front Street is Highway 47, and the speed limit is 55.

In fact for some, that's about all Gaston was known for. A long-haul truck driver had a hard time remembering where Gaston was back in 2004 when I told him I lived in Gaston. "Gaston, Gaston ..." he mused, "I know I've been through there, but ..."

The people of Gaston are modest and do very little to draw attention to themselves. There are no signs, no banners, no markers touting the town's rich and fascinating history. It's not like people wouldn't see those signs if they were there, either. People do notice such things, even when they're going 55 in a 30 mile per hour zone.

Take my friend the truck driver, for example. "Oh yeah," he said suddenly, "It's on Highway 47! You go past a sign that says 'Welcome to Gaston,' then a cop says 'Here's your speeding ticket.'"

Gaston is so much more than that, of course, and speed traps have become rare. Shoot, the town always has been more than that, especially for a few years in the early part of the last century. A story in the June 8, 1916 *Oregonian* extolled the virtues of the "progressive little town," which boasted hotels, restaurants and a booming retail trade, including McDonald's, which billed itself as "Gaston's largest and best" department store.

Back then, people like *The Oregonian* reporter appreciated just how great a place Gaston is … although he did end his praise with "even though it compels motorists to 'Slow Down To Four Miles An Hour.'"

Trading Dobbin
for a Dodge

In 1916, most folks in Gaston fought their way across the area's bumpy, rutted roads with horses. Even the few early automobile enthusiasts often had to rely on horses, if only to pull their cars out of the mud, and many of Gaston's stodgy rural stock still scoffed at the automobile.

Gaston wasn't really that far behind the curve, however, because 1916 also was the year that the first tank was introduced into World War I. Until then, the world's armies had fought their way through battlefield trenches mostly on foot and horseback. In 1916, even many of Detroit's great industrial pioneers hadn't fully jumped on the automotive bandwagon.

Take Horace Dodge, for example. By 1916, Horace was a rich man. He had, after all, invented the dirt-free ball bearing, a critical element in allowing cars to maneuver the country's dusty dirt roads. Horace had not invented the ball bearing with cars in mind, however, but rather for another modern marvel, the printing press. But that's not to say that Horace wasn't an early adapter to modern transportation. He and his brother were all over the new-fangled bicycle when it came to America in the late 1800s.

Living in Detroit, it was only natural that Horace would benefit from the rise of the Motor City, and he did so by branching into building motors for people such as Ransom Olds and Henry Ford. When World War I came along, the country needed all the industrial might it could muster to build motorized weapons to match the inventions of Britain, France and Germany. Horace Dodge did his part by building ambulances for the war effort. Finally in late 1917, Horace Dodge decided that maybe there really was a consumer market for these gizmos, and he sold his first automobile to the American public.

So if it took one of Detroit's great pioneers until 1917 to finally go all in on the automobile, one can't be too harsh on Gaston's great pioneers to do the same. Take, for example, Joseph Bates, who one might say actually beat Dodge to that conclusion, if only by a few months. By 1917, Joseph Bates was 92, and had never traveled by automobile. It's not as if Joseph Bates hadn't traveled, either, because he had. Oh, had he ever.

Joseph Bates came to the Oregon Territory from Vermont as a young man, but he remained fiercely devoted to his mother and sisters, whom he had left behind there. He was delighted when gleaming new steam-powered ships made ocean travel much faster, enabling him to visit his family back in what he referred to as "The States," despite the fact that by then Oregon had been a state itself for a full five years. Apparently Old Joe was sometimes slow to adapt.

He set out in January 1864 on a steamer out of Portland. Well, technically he didn't leave until February 3, because his ship had run into another steamer in the port, so his trip was delayed. We know all this because luckily for all of us, Joseph Bates kept a detailed diary of the amazing adventure he was about to embark upon. Finally on his way, he sailed 60 miles up the Columbia on his long journey when the ship he was on ran aground. The tide lifted the ship overnight and the next morning they were on their way for real.

Joe didn't sail all the way to Vermont on that ship, however, but rather only to Panama, where he crossed the isthmus to the Atlantic. Of course this was long before the Panama Canal, so he had to cross on land. He hadn't brought with him one of his trusty old Oregon farm horses (or "dobbins," as they were called) and there were no cars back then; in fact, it would be 20 years before people such as Horace Dodge brought even bicycles to the continent. So Joseph Bates walked across the mountains to his ship on the other side. From Panama he steamed up the coast to New England and saw his beloved mother once again.

He decided he didn't want to make the return trip to Oregon by steamer, so he began the 3,000 mile journey back home by train. He stopped in Dodge's native Michigan, albeit four years before Horace was born and more than 30 before the automobile's birth, and spent several weeks in Detroit visiting family. Finally in Iowa, one-third of the way home to Oregon, Joseph Bates decided he wanted a different mode of transportation, so he bought two mules and rode the remaining 2,000 miles across the Plains and over the Rockies and Cascades, mostly alone but joining with wagon trains whenever there were rumors of Indian ambushes.

Anyway, the point is that Joseph Bates had always gotten around just fine without an automobile. But then in February 1917, his friend John Baxter showed up at the Bates' home in Gaston, driving a car. It's not surprising that

Baxter would be susceptible to fads, because he was much younger than Joseph; Baxter was only 84.

"Why not trade off old Dobbin and get you a car, too?" Baxter asked his friend. We know all this because luckily for all of us there was a correspondent for *The Oregonian* present at the meeting. "It's a good idea, John," Joseph Bates replied. "I'll do it!"

His decision did not sit well with his family, however, who had some "consternation" about the image of Joe Bates learning to drive at age 92; they didn't want him to kill himself with an automobile after the rich, full life he had led. Family members kept an eye on Old Joe, concerned about him "falling victim to a fast-talking car salesman." Fortunately for the Bates family, there weren't a lot of car salesmen in Gaston in 1917, and even the fastest talker among them would have to be "one with a very loud voice" to close the deal with the nearly stone-deaf Bates. We know all this because luckily for all of us, his granddaughter Inez Porter Johnson wrote about it for the Washington County Historical Society in 1976. The family prevailed, and Joseph Bates never did drive a car, although he did nearly kill himself with one.

Walking out to see the new automobile bridge over the Tualatin River one morning, Johnson tells us, Joseph Bates, oblivious to the aahoooga of automobile horns, walked right into the path of "a Model T, which knocked him down and dragged him around, scraping the hair and flesh away from his skull and leaving the bone visible." The doctor said he would surely die, either from the injury or from the resulting shock. But "live he did," his granddaughter tells us, and "the hair grew back on his scalp as thick as ever. Grandfather was a hardy man."

But Grandfather Bates never bought a car. A few months later, back in Detroit, Horace Dodge and his brother John sold their first car, most likely to a much younger man, no older than, say, 84.

John Dodge, it is said, was a very fast-talking salesman.

Burn, Boom and Bust:
Gaston and Its Trees

Ignore Gaston. Just about everyone else does.

Take the Native Americans; only a veritable handful saw the promise of the rich soils and fertile hunting grounds around Wapato Lake. Most migrated west to coastal salmon habitat or east and south to the broad plains of the Tualatin and Willamette valleys.

Most white pioneers overlooked the area as well, again choosing the lush valleys to the east of the rugged Chehalem Mountains and Coast Range foothills. The railroad and highway builders likewise focused on more profitable routes up and down the valley and along the Columbia to the Coast.

Even in today's booming wine industry Gaston gets overlooked. A few miles north, Forest Grove lays dubious claim to being the birthplace of Oregon Pinot Noir, and the wine country that stretches from Gaston through Yamhill to Carlton is officially the Yamhill-Carlton Viticultural Area, somehow ignoring poor Gaston, whose wineries produce some of the region's best wines.

Only one group of people has consistently seen the value of Gaston and its steep valleys. Those people gaze up the Patton and Scoggins valleys and see visions of grandeur in the form of the cedar, spruce and Douglas fir stretching further than the eye can see, up and over the mountains to the Pacific Ocean. Over the years that group has included timber barons, aircraft engineers, shipbuilders and even Japanese military leaders, who placed bulls-eyes over Pearl Harbor … and over the hills around Gaston.

To early timbermen, the Patton and Scoggins valleys looked like superhighways into the vast, otherwise nearly inaccessible virgin forests. The superhighways allowed logs to be hauled to Gaston and put on trains and trucks for a smooth ride to Portland's rail lines that carried timber to the Midwest and or to the Rose City's deep-water port that sent logs and lumber on their way to the entire world.

The best-known among those timber barons were August Lovegren and C.W. Stimson, one known for his spectacular failure, the other for his spectacular success. But there have been many others through the years who have made careers both grand and humble from the forests. For example, Laurelwood and the tiny valley it sits in once was home to at least seven working sawmills and a large furniture factory, all fed by the dense forests.

Yet even Gaston's timber industry is often ignored, except when disaster looms. August Lovegren broke ground on his Cherry Grove mill to great fanfare, only to open it just as a tariff war with Canada ended, sending the price of logs plummeting. Still, his operation was so modern and strategically located he would have survived, if not for the torrential snow and rain storms of the Winter of 1913-14 that wiped out his dam and mill almost before he got started.

Other timber barons sat up and took notice of Lovegren's disaster. To them, his tragedy looked like a golden opportunity. The dam and mill were gone, but the railroad he built up the valley was intact, inviting others to pick up the pieces. New owners rebuilt on his old land but lacked the resources to thrive. Meanwhile, Stimson was quietly gobbling up forest land with plans to build the Northwest's greatest mill. He, too, coveted Lovegren's infrastructure along the Tualatin River, but couldn't agree to a price with Lovegren's successors so instead turned his attention one valley north, along the banks of Scoggins Creek.

Lovegren's plans had been expected to usher in a Golden Age for the Gaston area before tragedy and bad timing extinguished his nascent dream. Twenty years later, Stimson's plans for the Scoggins Valley ignited the same sort of excitement, if not more. After all, Stimson had even deeper pockets than Lovegren and the economy was booming like never before, driving demand for timber ever higher. This time, nothing but complete economic collapse or catastrophic fire could ruin the dream.

Chances of an economic collapse seemed non-existent, given the roaring Industrial Age growth of the 1920s. Even if the domestic economy did hit a bump, Stimson could exploit a new market Lovegren could not have foreseen: high demand from the defense industry for the light wood needed for airplanes. The firs, spruce and cedar fit that bill perfectly.

Chances of a raging fire seemed almost as remote. The heavy rains nine months out of the year kept the coastal forests moist and the many rivers and streams created natural fire blocks. Since settlers began logging the woods in the early 1800s there had been very few fires, and none that seriously threatened the vastness of this wilderness.

Add to those advantages the plentiful and incredibly cheap labor pool in the Gaston area. Agrarian by nature, the area had heretofore generated little organized labor or the kinds of conditions industrial workers in the Midwest and on the East Coast were coming to demand. The rugged farmers and loggers of the Gaston area were content with brutal conditions and modest paychecks. There was almost nothing that could ruin Stimson's dream.

Just before C.W. could even break ground on his state-of-the-art behemoth, Black Friday hit the New York Stock Exchange in October 1929, sending the economy into the Great Depression. Still, there was every reason to think he could weather the storm better than Lovegren had. The mill's modern design required far fewer workers than most, and the workers he did need came even cheaper now that other jobs were evaporating. Construction continued full speed ahead.

Soon Harold Miller, Stimson's son-in-law and manager of the Gaston mill, hit another snag that nearly derailed his plans. Stimson had built a rail line into the forests, but lacked a short spur to the rail line that ran through Gaston. This underscored the advantage Lovegren's site would have provided, because without a spur the mill was cut off from a vital link to the interstate rail network. He couldn't even get his locomotive, nicknamed "Peggy," to the mill. Stimson had applied to the federal government for a permit to build the spur, and as an alternative applied for a permit to move the locomotive by truck across state highways.

In *The Builder's Spirit*, a friendly biography of
Stimson and Miller, the authors pick up the story:
"Suddenly one morning 'Peggy' arrived, vines, limbs and
wires dangling from her stack and cab. (When) someone
asked Miller if he had been able to obtain a permit to move
the engine he pointed toward the track and said 'She's on the
track working.'" The authors leave one guessing as to
whether the law had been circumvented, but in reality it
probably didn't matter because of another secret weapon the
Gaston area possessed that made it a dream location for a
timber baron. Gaston is in Washington County. The county's
sheriff was John W. Connell, always a friend to
corporations, especially timber interests. A few years later,
his friendship paid even bigger dividends.

But reliable sheriffs alone are of little value to anyone
in the timber industry. What really set Gaston apart was the
magnificent forest to its west. The most magnificent stands
were across the crest of the Coast Range, but the central and
northern Oregon coast lacked a reliable deep-water port and
the rugged cliffs precluded adequate rail lines or highways.
Pulling log rafts to Portland was impossible because they
would break up crossing the treacherous Columbia River
Bar. Attempts to connect Yamhill to Tillamook along the
Trask River had been mired in politics and even violence.
Attempts to connect Forest Grove to Tillamook along Gales
Creek and the Wilson River had been mired in mudslides
and failures. The Wolfe Creek Road from Banks to Seaside,
now Highway 26, was still a pipedream in the 1920s and
'30s. The only known successful road over the mountains
had been one built by the Army during the Indian Wars from

Gaston to Astoria, but its exact route had been lost over the years.

Since the 1850s, loggers had tried to tap the forest's great potential with limited success, but it wasn't until Stimson tracked the old Army Road in the 1920s that Gaston became the regional nexus between the forest and the timber market. By the unbearably hot August of 1933, Stimson had built a rail line roughly corresponding to the old road and had his mill nearly ready to open. Yet once again, disaster would turn the timber industry's attention toward Gaston.

The disaster actually started a few miles north near Glenwood on Gales Creek. The hottest, driest summer in years gripped Oregon. The governor had closed logging on all state forest land, but the northwest corner of the state was nearly all privately owned. The official version of events says that Stimson and other responsible companies logged very cautiously, if at all, knowing a small spark could destroy their business. Other companies pressed ahead, desperate to eke out a living in the Depression. One such operator pulled two logs up a tinder-dry slope along Gales Creek on August 14, which created just such a spark, according to a commission established to determine the cause of the fire. The fire roared out of control, eventually "crowning," or racing into the tops of the tallest trees. When a fire crowns it sends ashes, embers, even entire blazing branches into the wind. Crews got the initial fire under control, but the embers from it had spread throughout the forest in the strong, dry east wind. Before long much of northwest Oregon, from about Carlton north and west to Tillamook and Seaside, was ablaze. The "Tillamook Burn" had become the worst forest fire in American history to that point.

Gaston became a focus of the disaster, but more for what didn't happen than what did. The nearly completed Stimson mill carried the hopes of the industry. Big enough to nearly out-produce all the other regional mills combined, it was a crown jewel that needed to be saved. Perhaps it was luck that saved the mill. Throughout the two-week inferno, no matter which way the wind blew it always seemed to blow the worst flames away from Patton and Scoggins valleys. But then again, perhaps it was more than luck that saved Gaston.

In 1933 there were few organized firefighting efforts in the forests. The timber companies did much of the fighting themselves. Stimson had the deepest pockets and arguably the most to lose from the fire, and the company spared no effort to preserve its interests. In the end, although the fire started just a couple of miles from Stimson property, the mill and much of the company's timber were saved. The Stimson men, as always, had performed heroically, although at a cost. Several were injured while fighting fires, and several, the authors of *The Builder's Spirit* tell us, "went berserk" in the raging inferno "and had to be locked in a tool shed."

Regardless, less than two months after the Tillamook Burn finally was extinguished, the Stimson mill opened to great fanfare. Not only had the fire not destroyed the Gaston mill, in some ways it had been a godsend. First, it had wiped out most of the smaller competition. Second, it had cleared the underbrush, making travel to remote areas easier than ever. Third, Stimson persuaded the state and federal governments to lift quotas, letting the company buy damaged trees at a fraction of their pre-blaze value. Some of the damaged trees still sizzled when they hit the mill pond in Scoggins Valley, and Stimson's fortunes sizzled along with them.

Everyone enjoyed the prosperity, except perhaps the brave local men who had built, saved and operated the mill. They still were laboring at about 43 cents an hour. By now mill workers around the state were beginning to go on strike, demanding higher pay and safer working conditions. The unions had shut down many of the mills in Clatsop and Columbia counties and set their sights on the giant Gaston mill. Unlike Washington County, however, Clatsop and Columbia counties lacked a sheriff like John Connell willing to use violence against his own people. For several years the strike was averted with force and the Gaston mill kept rolling out logs and profits for the Stimson and Miller families in Portland, Seattle, Palm Springs and elsewhere.

The mill muddled through strikes, the Depression and eventual unionization and by 1939 was poised to benefit from the economic recovery when disaster once again put the focus on Gaston. Yet another fire, again started near Glenwood by yet again a careless logging team, created another fiasco that rivaled the 1933 conflagration. This fire crowned and circled back toward Gaston from the southwest, coming within a mile of homes in Cherry Grove.

Stimson workers again joined the battle, but this time the federal government pulled out all the stops to help. This time national security was at risk. When the 1939 blaze began, America was not yet directly embroiled in World War II, but many of its allies already were or were about to be. The bountiful Oregon softwoods were in demand for military aircraft, and the shipyards in Portland relied heavily on wood and workers from the region. Soldiers from Fort Vancouver and other federal resources were brought to bear, with one objective being the preservation of the Gaston mill. This fire claimed some of the green timber spared in 1933, but once again didn't touch the mill. Gaston had dodged another bullet. Within a couple of years, however, it would be dodging something even bigger: Japanese bombs.

In December 1941, Japan bombed Pearl Harbor. For the next couple of years America took the war to the Japanese, putting them on the defensive in the Far East. But back in Tokyo, military leaders were planning an offensive against the mainland U.S.

Their plans didn't involve large-scale operations and didn't target Seattle or Los Angeles. Instead they targeted the area around Gaston, which by now had an air-raid lookout station staffed round the clock. First by plane and then by paraffin balloon, the Japanese military launched bombs they hoped would devastate Patton and Scoggins valleys.

First came the airplane, a disassembled float plane carried in a Japanese submarine off the Oregon Coast. One submarine, one small plane and a couple bombs might not seem like a ferocious arsenal, but in some ways this attack had more to do with terror than strategy.

The sub lingered off the Oregon Coast, twice surfacing for the crew to prepare the plane for its forays into

Oregon. Each time the plane dropped incendiary devices that touched off forest fires along the coast west of Gaston. The intended target was the timber on the eastern slope of the Coast Range, but the little plane and its pilot settled for drops closer to the coastline. The bombs did start fires, but they were extinguished quickly and not even attributed to Japanese attack until sometime later when bomb casings were found carrying Japanese writing. Later American intelligence services discovered the purpose of the attacks was twofold: to create terror in the homeland, and to start fires in the forests that would destroy material for planes and ships and divert military manpower to fighting fires. The failure of the mission was twofold as well. The blazes fizzled in the mist from the sea and the few people who reported seeing a Japanese warplane in the skies over Oregon were dismissed as paranoid, so no widespread terror ensued.

Next came the Japanese paraffin-balloon bombs of Project V1, which also targeted the forest lands of the Coast Range. For two years the Japanese floated the balloons when the jet stream was likely to carry them over northwest Oregon, equipped with timers to drop the attached bombs when they were likely to strike the Coast Range timber, setting off another conflagration.

Just as in the Tillamook Burn, Gaston got lucky. The bombs fell everywhere from British Columbia to Michigan, mostly landing unexploded and all missing their intended target. The forests around Gaston survived the onslaught. Sadly, however, six people enjoying a picnic more than 200 miles from the bulls-eye were not so lucky. A balloon fell

133

from the sky east of Klamath Falls near the California border. Elsie Mitchell and the five children she had taken on a picnic found the balloon and tried to drag it home. They didn't know it contained a bomb or that it still was live. The bomb exploded. Those six deaths were the only mainland fatalities of the war. But no timber, the bomb's intended target, was harmed in the blast.

Soon the war ended and Gaston again settled into obscurity. It's not that nothing was happening all around the town. Far from it. For years, thousands of ordinary Oregonians, including children in their yellow school buses, trekked into the forests west of Gaston to plant new trees to replace those lost in the Tillamook Burn. Logging companies both large and small went back into the woods to feed the nearly overwhelming demand for homes in the burgeoning post-war suburbs. Every day a steady stream of trucks brought logs to the Stimson Mill.

The mill even became a star of sorts in 2007, when the History Channel introduced the reality series "Ax Men." The first two seasons were shot entirely in the Coast Range forests. The mill was shown often, as were nearby timber towns such as Banks and Vernonia. Vernonia, particularly, enjoyed an economic boost from tourists flocking to see real-life loggers.

But the name of the town with the giant lumber mill and equally rich timber history was not mentioned once on the show.

No one in Gaston found the oversight at all surprising.

Gaston. Ski Country?

A century ago children in the Gaston area did things that today's children can only imagine, such as skating on frozen Wapato Lake, swimming in clear, deep creeks and skiing down the slopes of Patton Valley.

Mildred Krahmer, daughter of Gaston's first fire chief, remembered her childhood outings on the frozen water of Wapato Lake. "We'd have ice on there that would last for three weeks," Mildred told an interviewer for the Oregon Historical Society back in 1982. "We could build big bonfires out there on that ice and skate out there at night." Nobody skates on Wapato Lake anymore, but that's easy to explain: there is no Wapato Lake anymore. Even if the lake returns, our winters rarely get cold enough to freeze it.

The days of skiing in Patton Valley are a thing of the past as well, which isn't entirely a bad thing. Mabel Lovegren wrote about the time she spent skiing in Cherry Grove in the winter of 1913-14. The snow kept piling up and her brothers were kept busy in their mother's kitchen, steaming lumber from their father's mill to make it pliable enough to shape into skis. The mountains of snow were the children's delight but their father's worst nightmare; when a sudden January thaw hit, the dam Mabel Lovegren's father had finished the previous October couldn't hold back the melt and collapsed on its southern end. Mabel's father probably wished winters then were more like they are today, almost snow-free.

Still, Mildred Krahmer remembered those winter days with the same childhood innocence of Mabel Lovegren. Mildred didn't live out in Cherry Grove; she lived right in Gaston, up on the hill overlooking Wapato Lake. Her father had built a custom sled for her. "It was hickory wood and had metal on the bars and such. We tobogganed," she recalled back in 1982. "We had snow that would last for three weeks ..." The snow would pile up high enough that Mildred could ride her custom sled across several streets, then across the railroad tracks and right onto Wapato Lake. Or, on one occasion after church one Sunday wearing her best dress, she rode the sled right *into* muddy Wapato Lake, which wasn't quite as frozen as she thought.

Mildred also mourned the loss of many of the creeks from her childhood, a sentiment shared by Marge O'Rear, who grew up near the Lakeview School in the 1930s. Lakeview School is several miles southeast of Gaston and got its name because when it was built, Wapato Lake extended to within a couple hundred feet of its classrooms. By the time Marge arrived the lake had been drained, but she still had opportunities to swim in the two deep creeks that converged near the school, neither one of which exists as more than a trickle today.

The swimming is gone. The skiing is gone, too, and so is the sledding. "Oh, the weather's changed," Mildred Krahmer said. "Definitely."

Not All That Glitters Is Chicken Poop

There's gold in them thar' hills, those hills that rise from the edge of the valleys around Gaston. In fact, there's a rich vein up there that the Indians mined for many years, until they abandoned it because they believed it to be cursed.

At least we're pretty sure there's a treasure buried in that lost Indian gold mine up there. After all, we have countless tales of settlers watching the Indians bring huge nuggets out of the forest. And if we need more evidence than that, we also know chickens have a propensity to poop gold up in the hills around Gaston.

If only we knew where that chicken from old Bud Pennell's place in Dilley, just up the road from Gaston, ate the gold she pooped out in 1895, we all might be rich. *The Oregonian* reports a flurry of prospectors flocked (my word, not theirs) to Milton Dilley's donation land claim in search of the next gold rush after a chicken there passed some gold (one might almost call them "Chicken Nuggets"). But no one ever found where the little chicken discovered her gold, so no one got rich.

Lest you scoff at those eager Gold Rushers in Dilley, keep in mind that a mere six years later, another chicken touched off a smaller Gold Rush just on the other side of the Coast Range. This time, however, the expert avian prospector didn't get the glory she deserved. Thomas Whalen discovered these nuggets not in the chicken's poop but in her ventriculus, which also is known as the gizzard, one of the organs people dig out after killing the bird for food. That's how Thomas Whalen touched off another gold rush.

Old Tom bought a live chicken, not to eat but to use as flavoring for his clam chowder. When Old Tom cut apart the unlucky chicken to create broth, he discovered something shiny in its gizzard. Gold, old Tom said. Gold. Unfortunately, Old Tom's adventure was as fruitless as Milton Dilley's had been six years earlier. The Coast Range once again had dazzled but not delivered.

Apparently chickens are good prospectors, unless some create gold nuggets like oysters create pearls, because in the 1920s gold was found at least three times in hens on a chicken farm on the other side of the Tualatin Valley in Portland's West Hills. But that discovery did not spark a Gold Rush like the discoveries on Gaston's end of the valley did. In Gaston there are many hints besides chicken droppings that make prospectors' eyes sparkle.

Take, for example, M.F. Lake's 1948 discovery of chunks of glitter in the clay of his Patton Valley farm. But alas, all that glitters is not gold, and state geologists delivered bad news to Mr. Lake. After much fanfare and hope, it turned out that his "gold" really was mica. Still, many prospectors will tell you that where there's mica or quartz there's often gold, too, so the search went on in Patton Valley.

Twenty-five years earlier, just up the road near Carpenter Creek, four men had discovered real gold in what appeared to be an abandoned mine. Amid even more hoopla than old man Lake received, the men brought in heavy machinery to extract the treasure. Could this possibly be the lost Indian gold mine? Its location seemed to fit the sketchy directions better than Patton Valley, and the nuggets they found had been confirmed to be real gold. But forget the suspense; you already figured out these miners hadn't solved the mystery. They had found real gold and, as it turns out, a real abandoned gold mine, but it was one that white settlers had dug in the 1880s and abandoned for a very good reason; the scant quantity of gold it contained was not worth the time and effort needed to haul it out.

The quest for gold fueled much of the American West's growth. It seems like almost everyone harbored dreams of looking into a mountain stream, turning over just the right rock or stepping into just the right chicken poop, only to find a treasure in gold. In many ways, gold was a precursor to state-run lotteries; the odds of getting rich are astronomical, but that doesn't stop people from spending a lot of money trying. Like the lottery, gold-hunting tends to draw prospectors who have limited prospects for success in life. Prospecting lures adventurous dreamers and schemers and independent people who just don't want 9-to-5 desk jobs.

Gaston was built by such people, so it's no surprise that there are many tales of goldrush fever in these parts. But the people who built Gaston weren't dummies, either, and their dreams of gold had more than a little basis in reality. No one questions that the Kalapuyas had gold.

The tales of the lost Indian gold mine go back to the earliest days of white settlers in the area. Most of the tales concern Thomas Cornelius, a member of Oregon's first Senate after the creation of the state in 1859. Around Gaston, however, Cornelius is better known as the man for whom the small town between Forest Grove and Hillsboro was named.

Cornelius was a merchant by trade and ran the largest trading post in the region. Unlike many merchants, Cornelius allowed the natives to buy on credit. Legend has it that when their accounts grew too big to pay any other way the natives would ride up into the dense Coast Range mountains west of Gaston and return with large gold nuggets with which to settle their debts.

Legends abound of the Lost Gold Mine. All agree that white settlers would try to follow the Kalapuyas into the forest, but that they would inevitably lose the trail. In one version of the tale, a couple of white ruffians lay in wait for an Indian woman to return from the mine and tortured her for information on its location. In fact, this legend goes, the thugs tortured her until she died without revealing the location. At that her tribe concluded that the mine was jinxed and never returned. Yet another version claims that white settlers ambushed an Indian and his son upon their return from the mine, killing both for their supply of gold.

Perhaps the most well-verified versions come courtesy of Ruby El Hult in her 1957 *Lost Mines and Treasures of the Northwest* and 1971 *Treasure Hunting Northwest*. In her 1971 book, for example, she relates the story of William Perry, whose grandmother was a pioneer doctor near St. Helens, on the Columbia River. After his grandmother treated an elderly Native American, Perry related, the Indian held out a jar of gold from which to pay her. When she asked him where the gold came from, the Indian pointed toward a prominent notch in the Coast Range mountains, in the general area of Forest Grove and Gaston. Unfortunately, the old Indian's directions, "three walks, two sleeps," didn't pinpoint the exact location. Perry said his grandmother later pointed out the notch to him, and he recalls seeing the first Tillamook Burn start in the same place years later.

But the best-known story comes from Ruby El Hult's 1957 book and stars Sol Emerick, a farmer from the Gaston area. Emerick's story is an archetype of the "kindly settler much beloved by the natives he displaced" genre. In it, Emerick had heard tales of the vast gold mine for years, but dedicated his life to the search only after a deathbed encounter with an aged Indian woman.

The ancient grande dame pulled Emerick close on her deathbed to whisper the location of the mine in return for his compassion in her final days. She whispered a broken-English cryptograph straight out of the Lone Ranger: "Go three suns from a white mountain. Where water runs to a lake in a black canyon, you will find it."

In retrospect it's hard to know if she was showing him kindness or trying to drive him crazy, because Emerick devoted much of the rest of his life to a fruitless search for the magical mine. Still, Emerick remained a steadfast believer in the mine's existence, having personally witnessed Indians paying with gold at Cornelius' store. His zealotry enlisted others to the search, including a young farmer named Frank Watrous. Watrous, we learn from descendants in a 1977 article in *The Oregonian*, became as obsessed as his mentor, Sol Emerick. In a story ripped from the pages of a 1930s adventure novel, Watrous is said to have walked 70 miles through the forest to interview an aged Indian woman about the mine's location.

According to Ruby El Hult's account, this dowager of directions might have been more precise than Emerick's muse, because Watrous traced her clues and, he claimed, found the treasure of the Lost Gold Mine ... or at least clues to its location. Whatever, Watrous was convinced he had found his prize, but his jubilation was muted by the realization that the mine was on private property, and that property did not belong to him. Watrous kept his secret, returning occasionally to gather new hints and evidence, hoping against hope that the property would come up for sale so that he could snatch it off the market and claim the untold fortune that lay just beneath the ground.

That's about where Ruby El Hult's narrative ends, but Bill Turner, a writer for *The Oregonian*, picked up the trail from there after talking to Frank Watrous' nephew, Don, for a 1977 story about the still-mysterious mine. I know what you're thinking, that if the mine still was a mystery in 1977, many years after Frank Watrous' death, he probably had not really found its location. However, your cynicism, appropriate as it might be, could cheat you out of a good story if you fall victim to it. We are, remember, talking about a gripping 1930s pulp-magazine adventure here.

Which brings us to August 14, 1933. Frank Watrous was out in the forest along Gales Creek, along the route the Indians had taken to the amazing treasure of the Lost Gold

Mine 80 years earlier. Frank was gathering evidence to prove that he had indeed unearthed the riches, still hoping the property might come up for sale.

Frank might have been a bit on edge, however, because just a couple miles away the Stimson Lumber Company was about to open the biggest and baddest lumber mill in the Northwest. The mill had the potential to turn the timberland in which he was standing to gold, in the figurative sense, driving the price of his prized parcel beyond his somewhat modest means.

Imagine Frank Watrous standing there at the site of this monumental discovery, sweating both from the long hike and from the potential loss of his prized possession to the Stimsons, who probably couldn't see the treasure for the trees. The Stimsons and the other lumber barons saw Gaston only for the riches it could sustain. A vein of gold can be exhausted in an instant, while the forests are forever, at least in the wet, temperate Coast Range west of Gaston.

But the forest was not wet and temperate on August 14, 1933, as Frank Watrous trekked through the woods. It was sizzling hot that day, as it had been for weeks in one of the worst heat waves ever to hit Oregon. Fearing fire, the Governor had earlier that day ordered all work to stop in the forests, but that word was slow to spread. A couple miles from where Frank was standing that afternoon, a logger gave the orders to pull one more load up the hill along the banks of Gales Creek, along the path that leads to hidden treasure, the path that Indians took to their mysterious gold mine. There were no innocents in the wilderness that day, that afternoon of August 14, 1933. Every last one of them knew

143

the risk they were facing in pursuit of treasure, whether from trees or gold. The temperature was soaring. The crackling of brittle bristles on the Douglas firs sounded like a distant fire in the warm breeze.

As the loggers by Gales Creek jerked that load up the hill, the chains sparked. In an instant the woods were on fire, just as officials had feared, and would burn for days in what remains one of the worst forest fires in American history. Some of the loggers and rangers fleeing for their lives found Frank Watrous along the way and helped him to safety. Watrous could have scoffed at the timber companies' follies, because this fire certainly proved that the treasures they sought in the forest were not guaranteed to last forever. His fortune, on the other hand, would survive, buried as it was in the cool Earth, safe from the flames.

The Tillamook Burn that began that day destroyed the fortunes of many logging companies, but it also destroyed Watrous' dream. No doubt the gold had survived, but the fire wiped out every landmark and trail he had established. It scorched the earth so badly it was unrecognizable even to the most-seasoned woodsman. When the rains eventually came the suddenly bare soil was washed away and landslides filled canyons and, no doubt, old mine shafts. Watrous never again was able to locate the treasure; it had been lost for a second time, and as the forests regrew they belonged once again to the loggers, not to Frank Watrous. Watrous didn't blame the loggers for his loss, however. At least he didn't blame the loggers everybody else did for starting the fire that destroyed his dream. The eccentric prospector insisted for years that the fire started at least five miles from the official point of origin. Most people just ignored that wild story like they did his story about finding the lost gold mine.

Watrous was just one of many people who have searched for gold, yet their quest has brought no treasure to Washington County … unless you count Johnny Porter's quest in the forests of California back in the 1850s.

Johnny was a teenager who wanted more adventure than his parents' tree farm in Oregon could provide, so he packed up and followed the '49ers to Northern California in search of gold. He didn't find much, if any, and returned home. He did not return home empty-handed, however, as explained in a 1959 story from *The Oregonian*. The story tells of his family's disappointment when Johnny returned home to Oregon with nothing but a bag of pine cones, not something that is in short supply in the area. Yet 150 years after Johnny's aborted prospecting expedition ended, his legacy lives on.

Johnny was a tree farmer and he knew that the cones he lugged home from California were not from your garden variety Douglas fir. These were cones he had scrounged from around the bases of Northern California's giant sequoia trees. He tended to the seeds until they sprouted and then nursed them into saplings. Soon he planted some on his family farm, on aptly named Porter Road, and elsewhere around the area. The majestic giants that surround the Washington County Courthouse are among the trees Johnny planted so very long ago. He never found gold, yet we treasure his efforts still today.

That's the thing about trees: They keep coming back, no matter how hard we try to destroy them. The trees west of Gaston came back and made the Stimson family wealthier than just about any prospector. Johnny Porter certainly never got rich, nor did Frank Watrous or any of the chicken farmers with gold-pooping hens.

But don't for one minute think that the Lost Gold Mine doesn't exist just because no one can find it. If it is out there it might be no more than a small cave, covered in landslide debris, blackberries and poison oak. To give you an indication of how hard the search for the mine could be, take a look at the famed Boos Quarry.

Back in the late 1800s the Boos Quarry was a veritable gold mine. In its heyday the mine was a huge operation in Scoggins Valley, yielding majestic granite used in some of the grandest buildings in Oregon, including Portland's Pioneer Courthouse, the Washington County Courthouse, Marsh Hall at Pacific University and stately buildings at the University of Oregon and Oregon State University.

A century later, in 1975, a fire gutted Marsh Hall and burned so hot and for so long that even the granite cornerstones were damaged. Determined to rebuild the structure to its original glory, the university wanted to ask the current owners of the quarry for new stones. The search for the new owners hit an immediate snag, however, when no one could remember the location of the quarry, last mined in 1890. Eventually, after a well-publicized search, the quarry was found and new stones were excavated. Marsh Hall was restored to its original splendor. Happy ending all around, except recent searches for the quarry have again come up empty. It's out there; a huge hole in the ground, probably covered in blackberries and poison oak. Yet it's not easy to find, so just imagine how well hidden that old Indian gold mine is, if it's really out there ...

Any day now a chicken might deposit another clue or a logger might stumble upon a hidden mineshaft, somewhere in the hills west of Gaston, between the valley and the sea, and once again we could find ourselves in a new Gold Rush.

Hey! Has Anyone Here Seen Crater Lake?

Crater Lake is perhaps Oregon's most iconic landmark, made famous the world over in pictures by some of America's greatest photographers. Millions of people from all over the world have visited Oregon's only national park.

Most of those millions have visited the lake since about 1950, when the remote Oregon roads were improved enough to make visits by car practical for the average person. Until then, even most Northwesterners knew Crater Lake only through pictures. And the images that hundreds, perhaps thousands, of Oregonians and Washingtonians had of the lake were from paintings by a Gaston artist named Edward "Red" Earle.

Red Earle was born in Illinois, but came to Oregon in 1912 and never left, although he rarely settled anywhere for too long. "A lot of people called me the tramp artist," Red recalled in 1948, "and I guess I was. When I'd been in one place a while I'd gather up my brushes and move on." For more than 30 years the prolific artist kept moving until he had painted murals on the walls of cafes and taverns in nearly every town in the state until settling down in Gaston. His favorite subject was Crater Lake, which he painted on everything from giant walls of community halls to tiny shells of clams gathered along the beach at Rockaway.

His biggest project was the Gaston Community Center, an Army surplus building acquired at the end of World War II and rebuilt in what now are the baseball fields of Brown Park. To dress up the otherwise drab building, Earle's adopted hometown commissioned him to cover the insides with scenes of Oregon including, of course, Crater Lake. His images of the lake also at one time were on the walls of all of the town's diners and taverns.

But times change, and all of his Gaston artistry is gone now, as are most of his other works around the Northwest. Today, Crater Lake is an easy day's drive for most people in Oregon, so they don't need to rely on Red Earle's images of the beloved landmark, which is a good thing.

You see, Red Earle's travels as an itinerant artist took him to almost every town in Oregon, but he confessed to Ellis Lucia of *The Oregonian* that his journey never actually took him to Crater Lake itself. The images so many thousands of people saw throughout the Northwest all were conjured in the vivid imagination of a little "tramp" who finally found a home among the people of Gaston.

Nihilists, Nazis and Spies ... Oh My!

Gaston could be Anytown, U.S.A, with its collection of hardworking farmers, loggers, mechanics and your occasional Nazi leader or globe-trotting, communist-hunting spy ...

The town is full of familiar faces with names that go back generations in the area. Strike up a conversation and you're likely to hear stories of Scoggins Valley before the dam, trips in school buses to reforest the Tillamook Burn, or of the days when Laurelwood was littered with lumber mills. But today you probably won't hear any stories of intense personal conversations with Adolf Hitler or of years spent behind bars in China. At least if you do hear such stories today, you can bet at least most of them aren't true.

Things were different back in the 1940s and '50s. Back then you might have heard such stories, and they would have been true, or at least some of them ...

Imagine striking up a conversation with a humble farmer on a field west of Gaston only to hear: "Yes, I was a Nazi. Do not be shocked." That's what a reporter for *The Oregonian* heard one day in 1948. Or imagine driving a few more miles west to Cherry Grove in 1955 to listen to Levi Lovegren share tales of living through the devastating dam break in 1914, or of his missionary trips to the Far East, or of his imprisonment on spy charges, or how he was front page news around the world while diplomats from many countries worked for his release from a Chinese prison as part of a spy swap.

Levi Lovegren's headstone tells part of his story: "My ambition: To preach the Gospel where Christ has not been named. Missionary, builder, teacher. Sept. 19, 1888, to Oct. 6, 1983." Those words etched in granite barely scratch the surface of his amazing 95 years on Earth, however.

Levi's father, August, was each of those things as well, though he is best known as a builder, having built a spectacular dam, sawmill and in fact an entire town. He was a missionary to be sure, but his primary goal was not to go in search of disciples, but instead to build Cherry Grove as a lure for clean-living Baptists to come to him. Levi was at his father's side the entire way and carried on August's Baptist fervor long after the flood of 1914 swept away his Biblical dream.

August made his mark in Cherry Grove, but left when the dam burst and is buried near Seattle. His son, Levi, left Cherry Grove as well, but returned and is buried there. Levi's legacy was written in the years in between, in a place about as far as one can get from Patton Valley. Levi accepted his first missionary assignment to China in 1917, beginning a path that would lead him to the Baptist ministry. That path led him around the world, preaching the Gospel to anyone who would listen. By the 1940s, he landed with the Army Air Corps as a Chaplain during World War II.

Levi did more than just console and counsel aviators, however. Along the way he spent some more time in China, spying for the U.S. government, using connections he had made in his 14 years as a missionary in the country. His years as a spy behind the "Bamboo Curtain" went off without a hitch at the time, but soon would come back to haunt him.

By 1946 the war was over and Levi was living in Seattle, where he was approached to once again put his espionage to work in China, in a mission that could have been a prelude to the "Rambo" movie series. Levi was one of 12 people selected to scour the jungles along the border with Vietnam in search of WWII American prisoners of war rumored to be held by the Lolo tribe. The daring expedition was, at least officially, organized and paid for by the Conservative Foreign Mission Society of the Baptist Church. Levi Lovegren was named leader of the expedition. His force would consist of a nurse who had spent time in China and 10 freshly minted missionaries, none of whom had ever been to Asia. The expedition would not go well.

Before they could find any of the rumored POWs, the missionaries were captured by the Chinese government after the Communists learned of Lovegren's intelligence background. Lovegren vehemently denied that he still was an agent for the government. "They accused me of being an agent," he said later. "I was not. I am a missionary." The Chinese did not believe him, and so began five years behind bars in a Chinese prison.

Back in Cherry Grove, Levi's mother, Hilma, and two sisters waited for word from him. They wrote letters to the federal government, urging intervention on his behalf. Soon his capture was an international incident, but the Chinese refused to release him. President Dwight Eisenhower became involved, but because the American government did not want to talk to the Communists, his messages had to be relayed by diplomats from Britain and India. Finally a prisoner swap was worked out and headlines throughout the country announced Levi's imminent release. His release was not as imminent as his family had hoped, however, as China freed most of the others but held onto their prize, Levi Lovegren. Back in Cherry Grove, Hilma Lovegren died a few weeks before her son's release from his faraway prison.

Levi briefly toured, speaking of his experiences abroad, and in 1963 settled in his family home in Cherry Grove, where he lived until his death in 1983, to be buried beneath a headstone that doesn't begin to convey the true complexity of his life.

As complicated as Levi Lovegren was, however, his story is simple compared to that Nazi who lived down the road from Cherry Grove while Lovegren languished in prison. Hermann Rauschning was, by the time he moved to Gaston, already an internationally acclaimed author of several best-selling books about Hitler and the Nazis, including the authoritative *Hitler Speaks*, written from notes Rauschning kept while he was part of the Fuhrer's inner circle in the build-up to World War II.

Gaston would seem to be an odd place for Rauschning to live out his life, but that's exactly what he intended to do when he bought his farm in 1948, a few years after the Third Reich collapsed. He moved here, he said, because the countryside reminded him of his farm back in Danzig, where his long odyssey began back before the war, back before he and Hitler became pals.

Rauschning's rise in the Nazi party began after his heroic service for the German army in World War I. After earning a doctorate from the University of Berlin, Rauschning settled on a farm in Danzig and by 1933 had risen to the rank of president of the Danzig Senate. As a rising star in the Nazi party, Rauschning caught the attention of Hitler himself and he became a part of Hitler's inner circle. When der Fuhrer needed a personal envoy for talks with the president of Poland, he called on Rauschning.

According to Rauschning's account in 1948, he was under the impression that his role was to engage in good-faith negotiations with the Polish leader to settle differences with Germany. Instead, he told writer Ellis Lucia, when he went to Hitler with a plan for permanent peace with Poland, Hitler rebuffed him, telling him that "only one can rule" on the path to total world domination. Later, after Rauschning refused Hitler's orders to round up Jews, Catholic priests, Muslims, Gypsies and opposition leaders in Danzig, he saw the handwriting on the wall and fled Germany for exile in Poland. His flight eventually led him to the fertile soil of Gaston, but not before a decade with more twists and turns than the roads over Bald Peak, often with Hitler close on his heels.

When Hitler invaded Poland, Rauschning and his family fled again, this time to London, taking with him his handwritten notes from his meetings with Hitler, which he compiled into his best-selling *The Voice of Destruction*, a scathing warning to the world of Hitler's true intentions, which later was re-titled *Hitler Speaks*. From London, he came to the United States to urge a still skeptical nation to

154

take a stand against the Third Reich. His wife, Anna, took their children to Paris to wait out the war. Unfortunately, the Nazis soon were on the streets of France, and Anna and the kids fled yet again, this time to Portugal. Now separated from Hermann by an ocean and with children to care for, Anna wrote a best-seller of her own, *No Retreat*.

Eventually Hermann, Anna and the rest of the family were reunited in the United States, where they watched World War II spread through Europe from across the Atlantic Ocean. After the war they moved to California until on a visit to Oregon Rauschning fell in love with the area around Gaston, which reminded him of his beloved birthplace in Europe. In 1948 he packed up his family in Los Angeles and settled on a small farm in a valley just west of town.

Rauschning insisted he wanted to leave politics behind him when he moved to Gaston. Years on the world stage, including frequent exits stage left or stage right to evade pursuing Nazis, had left him craving the anonymity of the Oregon backwoods. He told *The Oregonian* in 1948 that he planned to live out his life quietly, tending to his crops on his little farm in Gaston. His message to the world, he explained, was to combat the nihilism spreading through Europe and to embrace instead the American Protestant spirit.

He was raised a farmer in Prussia and always appreciated the importance of hard work, a connection with the land and a love for family. His few years in Hitler's inner circle served only to reinforce that sense. Working the rich soils of Gaston, nurturing his crops and his children, was the culmination of his life's dreams. Life had meaning in Gaston, a community that always had relied on hard work, strong values and an abiding faith that better times are just around the corner. Rauschning seemed to fit right in, and it's no wonder he planned to live out his life here.

His plans soon changed, however, and within a few years he had moved to Southeast Portland, where he continued writing and lecturing until his death in 1982 at the age of 94. The reasons for his move are not clear, but in retrospect it's clear that his values didn't mesh with his stubbornly independent Gaston neighbors as much as they first appeared to.

In reality, he might have felt more at home with Charles H. Martin, the autocratic governor who in 1935 ordered vigilantes to attack strikers at Gaston's Stimson Mill and who also supported Hitler in the run-up to the war. Martin hated those he considered to be "Bolsheviks," which seemed to include almost anyone who didn't follow orders barked at them by their commanders.

Rauschning hated Bolsheviks as much as, if not more than, Martin did. In his works critical of Hitler, Rauschning had clumsily attempted to equate Nazism with socialism and communism. He fanned the flames of hatred for all three movements in an effort to restore a different kind of autocratic government, the monarchy, in Germany. Those who know Gaston probably would agree that there would be little support for a monarchy here. Rauschning's reactionary politics would be out of place among Gaston's historically live-and-let-live legions.

Still, it would be fun to be able to say that Gaston once was home to a member of Hitler's inner circle and world-famous biographer of the man, but to do so would be stretching the truth.

Not because Rauschning didn't live here, because he did. The real reason it would be stretching the truth is because it appears Rauschning himself stretched the truth. Maybe just a little, or maybe a lot.

His once-definitive *Hitler Speaks* now is regarded by experts more as clumsy propaganda than as a seminal work of the 20th Century. One such expert is Wolfgang Hanel, who contends that Rauschning never was close to Hitler and met with him no more than four times, and always as a member of large groups. Hanel further contends that large parts of *Hitler Speaks* were plagiarized, sometimes from works of fiction.

His ideological break from the Nazis remains somewhat in dispute as well, in part because Rauschning's ideology was never entirely clear. When he joined the Nazi party he was living in an area that had been placed under Polish control after World War I by the Treaty of Versailles. Rauschning railed against and cataloged instances of discrimination by the Polish against the German minority in the region. Fearing the Poles would take his farm, he longed for his homeland to regain control and saw the Nazis as his best hope. Ironically he would lose his holdings not to the Poles but to his Nazis when he disobeyed their orders.

In 1939, now penniless and a man without a country, Rauschning took his bitterness toward Hitler to Emery Reves, a French publisher who made *The Voice of*

Destruction an international best-seller. In a 1981 interview, however, Reves said Rauschning was most interested in a fat advance for the book. Even more damning, Reves said he and Rauschning mapped out what themes and traits to attribute to Hitler, and that he considered much of the book to be a complete fabrication.

By the time all this was known, Rauschning had departed Gaston. Just like the town's other famous author, Joseph Gaston, Rauschning's love affair with the town didn't last very long, with each preferring the lure of Portland's high society. But at least Gaston left a drained lake and a whistlestop with his name on it. Rauschning, unquestionably a witness of some of the world's most important events, left little trace in Gaston.

The Gaston area played very different roles in the lives of its two most famous World War II celebrities, who died only months apart, each in his 95th year. Levi Lovegren began and ended his amazing journey here, leaving his mark not just on a headstone in Cherry Grove but with his family's countless contributions to the community they loved.

At least we know how Levi Lovegren wanted to be remembered by the people of Gaston, but Hermann Rauschning's headstone leaves no such clues. Perched on a hill in Portland's most exclusive cemetery, with a view extending to the other side of the valley where Levi Lovegren lies buried, there's a slab of granite that reads simply: "Hermann Rauschning. August 7, 1887. February 8, 1982."

It's likely Rauschning didn't care what the good folk of Gaston thought. After all, he once wrote "The mass understood and understands nothing and does not want to understand." Of course that's not true, for while most of us don't understand the finer points of either nihilism or Nazism, we do understand why, in one of Rauschning's more lucid moments, he fell in love with Gaston.

Gaston really isn't just Anytown, U.S.A., after all. True, every town has a few garden-variety nihilists, even if some of them might not believe nihilism even exists.

But not every town can lay claim to having been home to famous Nazis and POW-hunting spies.

Gaston can.

The Year We Made News

Joseph Gaston was a newspaperman before moving to the town that would one day bear his name, including a stint as editor of the *Salem Statesman*, yet he never started a paper in Gaston and many of the events during his time here were never recorded.

Five years after his death, the town finally got its newspaper, *The Gaston Herald*. The paper lasted only months, but in its short life it helped paint a picture of life in rural Oregon.

"Emil Olsen has just been in town," we learn in one report. "He ran a nail in his foot last week but is nearly well now."

A nail in his foot is not what made Mr. Olsen's visit to Gaston newsworthy, however. The fact that he was even able to make the trip from his farm was the remarkable aspect of this gripping account. Olsen, you see, lived in Spring Hill. Spring Hill had been separated from Gaston by Wapato Lake and by the Tualatin River. Making the trip to Gaston in one of the early automobiles had been a nearly all-day journey through Forest Grove until 1918, when the lake finally was drained enough for construction crews to create a grade for a road between the two towns. The result was a road that "is a big thing for both communities," the *Herald*'s editors reported, and they routinely wrote stories about intrepid Spring Hillians who made the one-mile drive into town on what now is called Gaston Road.

But the *Herald* also reported other stories in its short existence, many of which concerned illnesses, often without much detail. For example, we learn that "C.W. Tucker is able to be around after a couple of weeks' illness," or simply that "Sam Baxter is quite a little better." As the year went on, the stories got a bit more specific, as when the town's doctor, J.A. Baker, returned from a conference in Denver to report "many cases of the influenza in Colorado and other eastern states."

Then the reports became more ominous: "Allow no visitors, and do not go visiting," and "Keep away from crowded places, such as the 'movies.'" But then the good news: "Miss Sarah Bates has returned to Portland to engage in teaching as the ban on the schools of that city on account of influenza, is now lifted." And then, "The Gaston school opened up Monday after a month's vacation on account of the influenza. We are glad to say none of the children were seriously troubled with it."

But others in Gaston were seriously troubled by the worst flu pandemic of modern times. "Mrs. Sam Koberstein passed away November 1 at her home south of Gaston, after a few days illness with influenza. She leaves a husband and five small children." The *Herald* ran several more flu-inspired obituaries, mostly just small items about women widowed without any means of support or families of young children left without mothers ...

In between were updates about Gaston boys deployed for World War I, late potato crops and of course the stories of visitors from far-off Spring Hill. But within a few months the *Herald* disappeared.

Who needs a newspaper when nothing of importance happens in a town like Gaston?

Bigfoot, Psychic Ghosts, Flaming Poo Balloons

In every American town, from New York City to Gaston, there are tales of dark mysteries, tales of ghosts and UFOs and strange beasts and people hiding dark, secret pasts.

Gaston is just your typical town. We have legends of UFOs; in our case involving flaming balloons containing foul substances dropped from strange airships. We have legends of people with hidden pasts; in our case involving world-famous conmen and odd little hermits who secretly own Norwegian shipping lines. We have legends of strange beasts; in our case, since we abut a dark forest, involving Bigfoot.

In the big cities such tales often are fueled by the news media and involve people or places most people don't know, a combination that gives the story some credence to people who want to believe and makes it nearly impossible to debunk for those prone to skepticism.

In Gaston such tales are fueled by gossip about, and from, people you see every day. People prone to believe such tales trust the story because they heard it from someone they know. But sometimes such rumors tend to fade faster in Gaston than in an urban center because they involve, well, precisely *because* they involve people everybody knows, or at least think they know.

Take our close encounter with Bigfoot. The year was 1964. The place was the far edge of Cherry Grove, at the very end of Lee Falls Road where civilization yields to the wilderness of the Coast Range rainforest. The evidence was stark: Blood-curdling screams and huge footprints in the mud. Add the frightened eyewitness accounts of local people, and the story warranted much gossip and accounts in local newspapers.

Consider our close encounter with space aliens. Fire rained from the sky over the Laurelwood Academy one frigid winter night. Students reported a spacecraft hovered overhead as balls of a strange, flaming, blue substance landed on the roofs of the buildings, suspended from balloons. The story might have been dismissed but instead made the pages of *The Oregonian* because the episode had another, more credible, witness: the school's dean of men.

For ghost stories, consider the strange saga of Louis Rader. When government agents swooped in to arrest him at his Gaston farm as a would-be Presidential assassin they had no idea that his case would take on a supernatural quality when his conversations with ghosts proved eerily prescient.

Then there are the stories of people with hidden secrets in their pasts, of which we have several. One such character was Eric Sandlin, an odd little man who lived a life of poverty in a shack by the muck of the onion fields but whose death warranted news coverage around the state because of the "amazing discovery of bank certificates, bonds, securities, foreign notes, papers and a raft of correspondence indicating that Sandlin controlled, or at one time controlled, a vast fortune."

Another character hounded by such gossip was a modest pastor assigned to the remote Cherry Grove Baptist Church, who supposedly was in fact a con man hunted by the FBI and Interpol.

As it turns out, some of these rumors are true, or at least have some basis in reality. Others, of course, are hoaxes, such as Bigfoot's visit to Cherry Grove. Still others, such as the saga of the Flaming Poo Balloons, are best filed away in a folder called "No One Really Believes This Crap."

People doubted the Bigfoot rumors from the start, but over time as evidence mounted, more and more people became concerned there really might be a monster in their midst. A story in the *Forest Grove News-Times* recounts an eerie, fog-shrouded night in March 1964. "Unnervingly," the *News-Times* recounts, "came a hideous scream that knifed the heavy night air. It could have been a prank or even just a dream, residents told themselves, and went back to sleep."

The next night was equally shrouded, equally eerie and equally shrill as once again the screams startled residents from their slumber. After four or five nights of this, Cherry Grove residents demanded action from the sheriff's office, either out of fear or annoyance. But without a body, without a missing person, without a known victim of any kind, deputies told the sleepless citizenry there was nothing they could do.

Then, about a week into the drama, the situation took a new turn. A group of teenagers out investigating the screams came across gigantic footprints in the March mud. The prints measured 18 inches by eight inches, and the stride of the monster placed the prints a full eight feet apart. The tracks suggested the monster had walked out of a field and into the woods ... and right through a sturdy wooden cattle fence, now reduced to a pile of splinters in the dewy grass.

The deputies now had a victim, if only a victim of a property crime, and they sent a detective out to investigate. Not surprisingly, police did not believe the scene was evidence of a monster stalking the good folks of Cherry Grove, but neither did they have enough evidence to file charges against any of Cherry Grove's more-human inhabitants. The entire drama remained shrouded in mystery and the fog of the late Oregon winter. The perpetrators of the hoax, assuming it was a hoax, had eluded detection. At least for the time being. It turns out they had made one critical mistake: They had destroyed a fence belonging to the wrong person.

The owner of the fence was Birgetta Nixon, a rugged backcountry woman unafraid of anyone or anything. The teenage boys might have stymied the detective, but Birgetta didn't have to play by the rules of the American judicial system and it didn't take her long to elicit a confession, which she recounted in her 1976 book, *Cherry Grove*, including the names of the lads, each of whom she knew well and suspected of mischief. No more fences were crushed, and the monstrous screams of the night were silenced, along with the rumors in a small town.

If only Birgetta had lived on the other side of town, in the village of Laurelwood, we might have a definitive answer to the mystery of the Flaming Poo Balloons, but alas, we have no such resolution to Gaston's space invasion. Like the Cherry Grove Monster (or almost any horror story worth its salt), the Poo Balloon mystery unfolded in a cold night, shrouded in fog.

The night when terror rained from the skies, December 19, 1968, the Laurelwood Academy was a crowded place. Billed as the world's largest Seventh-day Adventist school, hundreds of students from throughout the nation and world lived and worked on the picturesque campus. On that Thursday evening, the thoughts of most of those students were on the celestial objects associated with the upcoming Christmas holiday, such as the Star of Bethlehem.

What some of them saw instead was something quite unholy: A spacecraft hovering over the boys' dormitory. When the attack began, when the aliens in the space craft began shooting flaming packages of blue poo at the boys, one of the students ran to summon the dean of boys, Ronald Turner.

Turner told police and a reporter for *The Oregonian* that the UFOs resembled parachutes from which burning objects hung, maybe 1,500 feet above the school. When one of the bright blue projectiles landed on the roof, Turner sprang into action. Well, he didn't actually spring into action himself, but he did order one of his charges, 15-year-old student body President John McChesney, to the roof to stomp out the flaming package.

Police reported no damage to the building, nor to McChesney. The evidence was destroyed and there's no record of concerned parents suing the school for using young boys to fight off an attack by alien space invaders. It's possible that Turner just didn't want to venture out on the roof on such a frigid night, or that he didn't want to surrender his command post in case further emergency orders became necessary to halt the invasion.

Of course it's also possible that Turner ordered the boys to handle the situation themselves because he knew or suspected the whole episode was a prank of their own making. Perhaps he involved the police to instill some fear in the impressionable students' hearts. Whatever, the story in the next day's *Oregonian* provided no insight into Turner's motives or opinions of the whole affair. Unlike the Cherry Grove Monster, there's no definitive explanation for the night flaming poo balloons lit up the skies over Laurelwood.

The motives of those suspected of hiding secret lives remain unclear as well. Why would a man live like a hermit in a decrepit shack if he really was a millionaire? Why would a man who lived a life of international intrigue suddenly turn up as pastor at an old wooden church in the foothills of Oregon's Coast Range? Why would a quiet rancher warrant a raid by federal agents?

The case of Louis Rader is the easiest of the three to solve. Rader was the subject of many stories in *The Oregonian* after his arrest, but the basis of his story is revealed in the cascading headlines on the very first article, which appeared on the doorsteps of Portlanders on the morning of June 27, 1923. The story involved a planned visit to Portland by President Warren G. Harding, and the main headline blared: "Farmer Threatens Life of President." The first subhead elaborated on the evidence against him: "Rancher of Gaston Arrested for Writing Letter."

On the surface, a letter threatening the life of a President about to visit the area sounds pretty damning. Upon closer inspection, however, the letter seems more a statement of confusion than confession. The letter was written to the Portland Chamber of Commerce and contains this threat, or possible threat: "Now friends this nice morning I have a hunch here it is President Harding will be called this month on a Fryday to a high court where he will give account to the above mention."

OK, so maybe the letter itself left a little doubt about his motives, but this is where Mr. Rader's small-town neighbors enter the drama. Rader is described as "a grizzled (sic) little German, short of stature, stockily built, with a cheerful, good-natured disposition." But neighbors told investigators of a darker side to this immigrant from Europe who, they said, was hiding a past as a radical in his faraway homeland of Germany. While he had managed to escape to America, neighbors said, many of his fellow radicals remained imprisoned back home, and he hoped to avenge what he saw as injustices perpetrated against them. Rader was, his neighbors in Gaston told the agents, much too dangerous to remain free while Harding was in the area. Another of the subheads in the *Oregonian* story summed up the neighbor's accounts: "Louis Rader, Elderly German, Who Is Said to Be Erratic, Forecasts Death of Harding."

Louis Rader, however, was never charged with any crime, freed in part by the meaning of the word "forecasts." The final subhead elaborates: "BLAME LAID TO SPIRITS." The spirits that led to Rader's arrest were not the kind being distilled in the steep hills of moonshine territory across the valley, either. They were "celestial spirits" who spoke regularly to Louis Rader, guiding every aspect of his life. It seems that while his nosy neighbors were speculating about him conspiring with radicals, he really was conspiring with unseen apparitions to lay bare the future. These spirits had sent him a prophecy that Harding would die in Portland.

It was ghosts, not Rader, who predicted this foul turn of events, but the Feds had no jurisdiction to arrest the ghosts so Rader was the one who found himself in jail. Rader's luck improved while he languished behind bars, however, when he got yet another message from his guiding spirits, telling him that they had been wrong about Harding's impending doom in the Rose City. Louis Rader shared the good news with prosecutors and was released to return home to Gaston.

Of course Warren G. Harding did not die on his visit to Portland, where he gave a triumphant speech to nearly 30,000 people at Civic Stadium on the Fourth of July before continuing on to British Columbia and then north to Alaska. He even visited Portland again on his return train trip, but this time he had to cancel a planned speech because he unexpectedly fell ill between Seattle and Portland. So no, Warren G. Harding did not die in Portland. He died a couple of days later in San Francisco from the sudden illness that thwarted his second Portland appearance.

Louis Rader was wrong on another count: Harding did not die on a "Fryday"; he died late on a Thursday night. Nonetheless, Rader felt vindicated and a few days later wrote a letter to *The Oregonian* from his farm in Gaston. In it, he said: "You know now I did not miss it very much."

We don't know if Louis Rader ever was an agent provocateur as his nosy neighbors alleged. Regardless, it wasn't his life before arriving in Gaston that made him interesting. It was his life on his little ranch that earned Louis Rader a spot in history.

The opposite is true for another of Gaston's mystery men, Ferdinand Waldo DeMara. Nothing Fred, as he was known by his neighbors in Cherry Grove, did while living in this neck of the woods was very interesting. The life he was trying to leave behind when he arrived in Gaston, however, was extremely interesting.

Fred DeMara was welcomed to the area in 1968 when he was named pastor of the Cherry Grove Baptist Church. The reverend was a big, jolly fellow with a booming voice and hearty laugh. His parishioners fell in love with him and he fit comfortably into the community.

Soon, however, rumors spread about DeMara. They were not pleasant rumors either, but instead accused him of being a world-renowned con man who had pretended to be a Navy surgeon, Trappist monk, prison warden, civil engineer, lawyer, Benedictine monk, child psychiatrist and more.

At first, the Reverend DeMara's parishioners in Cherry Grove scoffed at the rumors and defended him as a pious, caring man of the cloth. The truth, they knew, would set him free.

Instead the truth turned out to be that Ferdinand Waldo DeMara was the one who had been set free, released from prison not long before arriving in Gaston. His offense? Impersonating a Navy surgeon, Trappist monk, prison warden, civil engineer, lawyer, Benedictine monk, child psychiatrist and more.

The good folk of Cherry Grove had no reason to be embarrassed if they felt fooled by their new pastor, who had fooled much more-sophisticated audiences. He was, after all, quite possibly the greatest con man ever. He was a con man worthy of a hit 1961 movie called "The Great Impostor," starring Tony Curtis as DeMara. He was hunted by the FBI and Interpol and immortalized by Bob Dylan and The Band in a song called "Ferdinand the Impostor." Much later, he became the inspiration for the 1996-2000 NBC series "The Pretender." DeMara was not your garden-variety impostor.

Still, while audiences influenced by the mass media were quick to write off DeMara as a fraud, those who knew him in the small town of Gaston gave him a second chance. Cherry Grove's cynical maven, Birgetta Nixon, had nothing but kind words for the Great Impostor who, she says, "was exceptionally well-liked here." The DeMara of the Cherry Grove Baptist Church did not seem to be someone trying to pull the wool over anyone's eyes; instead he seemed only to want to lead his flock as a shepherd of the Lord. After leaving prison, he had earned his degree, fair and square, in 1967 from Portland's Multnomah Bible College and eagerly accepted his assignment to lead the Cherry Grove church as his first ministerial assignment. He didn't last long in the Gaston area, but his role as a fire-and-brimstone preacher proved to be his last persona, one that he pursued at other small-town, conservative Baptist churches in the Seattle area until his death in 1982.

The lyrics of "Ferdinand the Impostor" do a good job of capturing the thoughts of many Gaston residents who knew the subject of the song personally: "A voice just said he's not for real, but it's just his game and he carries no shame because he done nobody wrong ... (but) he knew he didn't belong." Although really, simply doing nobody wrong often secures one a sense of belonging in the hearts of Gaston residents.

Eric Sandlin, for example, was an odd man but accepted by his Gaston neighbors, even before they learned that he was (or at least might once have been) a multi-millionaire. No one ever made a movie of Eric's life, nor did he ever claim to speak through spirits. He probably never saw Bigfoot or a UFO, living as he did "in a ragged little trailer house down near the onion fields," as a story in *The Oregonian* of September 1, 1948, tells us. Eric Sandlin kept to himself, but still managed to capture the hearts of many in Gaston. And although Sandlin never captured the attention of Tony Curtis or Bob Dylan, he did manage to attract his share of media attention in the last year of his otherwise seemingly uneventful life.

In fact, stories about him appeared in the *Forest Grove News-Times* and on the front page of *The Oregonian,* not once but twice, in the spring of 1948. The stories chronicled Sandlin's running, or, more precisely, walking feud with a man named Ike Larson. On April 25, Harold Stassen and Thomas Dewey were in Portland, battling each other for the Republican presidential nomination, but their pictures were not on Page 1 of Oregon's largest newspaper.

No, instead that honor went to Eric Sandlin and Ike Larson, in a story about their feud in sleepy little Gaston.

The dispute, author Ellis Lucia explains, was "intersectional. Ike lives on the Gaston heights. Eric lives on the flats across the tracks." As in many Western towns, "the flats" were prone to flooding and the favored route for noisy, smelly railroads, so "across the tracks" was code for "the wrong side of the tracks." People who could afford to preferred to live up hill from the noise and pollution, in houses from which they could quite literally look down on poor people such as reclusive little Eric Sandlin. The origin of Sandlin's spat with Larson is unclear, but it escalated to the point that reporters from several newspapers came to town and "took Eric into enemy territory up on the hill," where the two men decided to settle their differences with a foot race. Given that Sandlin was nearly 70 and Larson was 82, the race would be of the walking variety.

The race was slated for the day the story ran, scheduled in conjunction with the town's major sporting event of the year, the Tualatin-Yamhill Valley League baseball game between another set of bitter rivals, Gaston and its neighbor a few miles to the south, Yamhill. A starter's pistol would signal the racers to set off to the finish line at home plate of the baseball field before the game began. Townspeople pledged to raise money for a cash prize for the winner, hoping to raise a dollar. Excitement ran so high, however, that the final jackpot reached $2.50, which didn't even count the many private bets being placed around town.

The next day, Sandlin and Larson were back on Page 1 with the results of the race, which, to put it mildly, didn't go well for Eric Sandlin. Ike Larson was the one who got off to a rocky start, because he was too deaf to hear the starter's pistol. But after a couple of false starts, the official switched to hand signals to get things going, and the race belonged to the older, but much taller, Ike Larson. Larson, we're told, jumped out to such an enormous lead that he walked backwards, taunting Sandlin to keep up with him and at one point dragging the hapless Sandlin by his arms. Ike Larson won the prize money to the loud cheers (which he couldn't hear) of the crowd at the baseball game and journeyed back up to the heights. The dejected Sandlin, who could hear every taunt and laugh at his expense, retreated to the flats, where he spent the rest of the summer of 1948 fishing, doing odd jobs and collecting junk in his humble home permeated with the smell of onions, returning to the obscurity he seemed to crave.

In early August, Sandlin was fixing to go fishing at the river when he fell and broke his collarbone. With no one in Gaston to care for him, his only known relative, his daughter Mabel, made the drive down from Kelso, Washington, and took him back to her home. He never returned to Gaston, because about a week after arriving at Mabel's house he had a heart attack and died. Mabel buried him in Kelso. But while his life in Gaston had ended, the stories about that life had just begun.

About his only real friend back in Oregon had been a man named Sam Williams, "a state varmint hunter who owned the trailer" in which Sandlin lived. Back in the onion fields, Sam Williams began the sad task of clearing the debris of his friend's life. He found little of interest until he opened an old steamer trunk. He could not believe what he found. Eric Sandlin, who had lived in pungent squalor on the edges of Gaston, owned at least a share of a Norwegian steamship company and, from the items in the trunk, appeared to be worth millions of dollars. Williams, the state varmint hunter, had no idea what all the financial documents meant, so he bundled everything up and called Mabel in Kelso with the good news. She was, he told her, rich beyond her wildest dreams.

We're not sure what Mabel's wildest dreams were, but we know a little about the imaginations of some folks in Gaston in the summer of 1948. They had cheered for Larson and laughed at poor little Eric Sandlin in the great walking race, but now the shoe was on the other foot. Apparently they had Sandlin all wrong; he was no tramp, but rather a reclusive millionaire. Word of his hidden treasure spread like wildfire through the town, soon capturing the imagination of the reporter in Portland who covered the fateful race a few months earlier. This story told of the "amazing discovery of bank certificates, bonds, securities, foreign notes, papers and a raft of correspondence indicating that Sandlin controlled, or at one time controlled, a vast fortune."

Williams packed up the trunk and sent it to Mabel in Kelso, while the people of Gaston eagerly awaited updates on the man who, in death, had become the town's most famous citizen. Neither Mabel nor Williams could read all the documents because they were written in Norwegian, so experts from Portland were called in to decipher them. The reporters awaited word as well, and regularly called Mabel for updates. Finally, she gave an update to one such scribe: "We have often heard people sometimes had quite a time proving they were heirs to a fortune, but we are certainly having the same trouble proving the opposite."

It turns out Sandlin had indeed owned a share of the Norwegian steamship line. In fact, he owned exactly a share, as in one of thousands or perhaps millions of shares. He owned just one share, which paid him about $36 a year in dividends. He also had wads of now worthless European currency and a lot of other things that were of value to him but not to the experts who examined them for Mabel. Still, rumors flew among the people of Gaston about the secret tycoon who once had walked among them, albeit too slowly to beat an 82-year-old man in a foot race. They wanted to believe the stories, but Sam Williams knew better. "It just isn't so," he told *The Oregonian*.

The people of Gaston apparently had known the real Eric Sandlin after all; there was no hidden treasure. They were right about Louis Rader as well, at least about his "erratic" nature; whether he actually talked to ghosts, on the other hand, is a matter of some dispute. They might have been among the few who actually knew the real Ferdinand Waldo DeMara; if, in fact, there was a real side to the man. They knew the culprits behind the Cherry Grove Bigfoot sighting much too well to put credence in their story. The folks of Gaston didn't really know most of the people at the Academy tucked away in Laurelwood; most weren't from these parts, so it's tough to know if their tales of flaming poo balloons falling from the sky had any merit.

In short, people in small towns really are pretty good at discerning the truth about strange rumors and legends because they know so much about the lives of their fellow residents.

Or at least they think they do …

Tillamook? Just go Straight at Idiotville

The town of Gaston is what it is today because of its strategic location near several well-known natural formations, including Wapato Lake, the Tualatin River, and the steep, forested Patton and Scoggins valleys.

But a full generation before there was a town of Gaston there was another town a mile or two south, a town named Wapato. Wapato was named not so much for the lake as for another natural formation that at the time was far more strategic than any other in the area, the Wapato Gap.

The small gap between the towering Chehalem Mountains to the east and the rugged Coast Range mountains to the west goes mostly unnoticed today as motorists cruise along Highway 47 between Gaston and Yamhill. Generations ago gaps of this sort were critical because crossing mountains was very difficult by stagecoach and even more so by train. Gaps, like the one called Wapato, were critical to our ancestors, but we hardly notice them today because we no longer need natural passages. We can overcome any obstacle and build transportation corridors anywhere we want to. Almost.

The founders of the town of Wapato recognized the strategic value of the gap and opened a store there, knowing that every traveler between the Yamhill and Tualatin valleys would have to pass right by their doorstep. Then, long before the people of Gaston had theirs, Wapato had a school and a

Post Office. Things looked even more promising for the folks in Wapato when plans for the Westside Railroad were announced, because the tracks had nowhere to go but right through the little gap called Wapato.

But the owners of the Wapato Store didn't own the rights to build the railroad. Joseph Gaston did. Nor did they own the rights to drain Wapato Lake. Joseph Gaston owned those, too. Joseph Gaston also owned the rights to decide where to put a whistlestop for the trains passing through Wapato Gap, and he decided that it would be in a new town just north of Wapato, a new town he would call Gaston. Once the railroad was up and running stagecoaches rarely ran through the gap to stop in Wapato, and the town withered away. In contrast, by 1872, Gaston had its own school, its own Post Office, its own store, and some things Wapato never had, such as a train station, a hotel, a warehouse and a blacksmith shop.

Still, Wapato's little store managed to cling to life for a few years by serving the dwindling local population, and then got a new lease on life from an invention even more modern than the locomotive: the automobile. The only place to build a road for automobiles travelling between McMinnville and Forest Grove was right through Wapato Gap. Suddenly the Wapato Store added a gas station and was in the catbird's seat to capture northbound travelers before they got to Gaston.

By the time cars came along Joseph Gaston had left Wapato Gap and Wapato Lake in his rearview mirror and had moved on to Portland, but he had given the town that bears his name a huge head start over little Wapato. Within a few years, Joe Gaston's successors had succeeded in draining Wapato Lake enough to build roads across its dry bed and into the Yamhill Valley through another rival small town, Dewey. Then Wapato's new lifeblood, the automobile, was perfected by people such as Henry Ford, and what Ford giveth, Ford can taketh away. As mass-produced cars evolved into ever-more powerful machines, they could easily carry people not only across the dry lake bed to Laurelwood, but also up and over the Chehalem Mountains, which just don't seem so "towering" to today's generations. In the end, the car, which had seemed like Wapato's savior, just made it easier than ever to bypass the town.

With car traffic dispersed, neither Dewey nor Wapato had enough to survive. Dewey died first, then Wapato. The Wapato Store lived on life support long enough for many of today's generation to remember it, although with no trace of it remaining many can't recall exactly where it was. The railroad is gone, too, and many in today's younger generations don't know it ever ran through the Wapato Gap. Many don't even know the name "Wapato Gap." Technical advances have brought us to the point that mountains and lakes and such are no longer obstacles. We have come so far that gaps no longer seem to be of any strategic importance … at least until a Gaston resident wants to make a quick jaunt to Tillamook. When one develops a craving for an ice cream cone or some of Tillamook's world-famous cheese, a gap through the Coast Range would come in mighty handy.

Tillamook is due west of Gaston, only 30 miles away as the crow flies. Shoot … it's so close to Cherry Grove that one can practically sense the aroma of Tillamook's famous cow pastures. But while people have noses, we don't have wings. We rely on cars, and to get to Tillamook by car from Gaston one must go far to the north and across Highway 6 through the ghost town of Idiotville, or far to the south along Highway 18 and through Hebo and Beaver, trips that double or triple the 30 mile journey we could enjoy if only we had a gap. But we don't, or at least we haven't found one.

It's not that we haven't tried to find a passage to Tillamook. Previous generations tried their darnedest to find one, but to no avail. Some pioneers did find their way from Gaston to Tillamook, usually by accident. Take Thomas Sain, who went hunting with his dogs from his donation land claim, far into the imposing hills west of his farm in Scoggins Valley. His farm no longer exists, buried by the waters of Hagg Lake when Scoggins Dam was built. His name lives on, however, given to one of the creeks that feeds the lake. What we know today as Sain Creek ran down into his farm from the dense Coast Range forests, and he had ventured up into the hills along its banks on one particular hunting expedition.

This particular hunting trip in 1867 hit a snag when one of his prized hunting dogs ran off and didn't respond to Thomas Sain's calls. Sain went off to find his dog, and promptly got lost. Sain kept searching for his pooch and then began searching for civilization, which was not easy to find up in those dark hills back in 1867. Eventually he heard voices and realized he had stumbled upon a town. To his surprise, however, the town he found was not Wapato. It was Tillamook.

The whole story might have been nothing but a humorous anecdote, but the case of the lost hunter drew intense interest from the United States Army, which asked Sain to try to retrace his steps so the Army could build a supply road from Gaston, not to Tillamook but to its strategic Fort Clatsop, up the coast near Astoria. Sain retraced his steps the best he could, and the soldiers managed to carve out a primitive trail through the mountains, passing close to where a logging camp named Idiotville would one day stand, so named because it was said only an idiot would venture to such a remote outpost to log. Very soon, however, the Indian Wars ended and Fort Clatsop no longer seemed quite so strategic. The trail once again went cold.

There were other attempts to find a convenient passage to the coast, the most successful being the stagecoach line that dropped down into Yamhill. The route was brutal and treacherous. The trip often required an overnight stay at the Summit House, an inn deep in the Coast Range wilderness that, by all accounts, was not a place most people wanted to spend the night. A story from *The Oregonian* about a gloomy November day in 1906 illustrates why.

It seems that while innkeeper Pat Doney awaited the arrival of that day's stagecoach, his dog presented him with a human hand. Not sure what to do with the appendage, Doney kept it to give to the nearest thing his wilderness outpost had to an authority figure: the stage driver. When the coach rolled to a stop, "Mr. Doney produced the grewsome (sic) relic, which was carefully examined by the driver and all the passengers." The driver sized up the situation and expressed the opinion that the hand was from a man and that it had been ripped from the man's body by the dog. But the dog proved to be an uncooperative witness, and when he returned to the inn with another piece of the man's arm, he "ran under the house and refused to be cajoled into bringing it out, so that the second portion could be identified." The stage driver took the hand to be examined by authorities in McMinnville, stopping to ask anyone he met along the way if they knew of any deaths or missing persons. None did, and the severed hand remained a mystery. It's fair to assume the riders on that stagecoach probably wished there had been a nice flat gap through the mountains to speed their return trip to Tillamook, even if it meant spending a night in Idiotville.

Much of that old stagecoach road remains passable by car, but one needs a heavy-duty four-wheel-drive to make the complete trek through creeks and over rocks and logs that impede travel in the most remote stretches, so most motorists stick with the much longer but smoother established routes.

Today's engineers certainly have the skills to turn the stagecoach route into a modern highway. After all, past generations had accomplished much more ambitious projects in even more forbidding terrain. The current generation, however, faces obstacles their great-great-grandfathers didn't have to worry about. For one thing, there's much more concern about the impact on the environment today than when, for example, previous engineers had figured out how to drain Wapato Lake, way back in the day when stagecoaches were still stopping at the Summit House.

We've learned that just because we can transform nature doesn't necessarily mean we should, such as when we figured out that Wapato Lake served purposes beyond just breeding mosquitoes.

But really, environmental concerns are not the main reason today's engineers don't build a road from Gaston to Tillamook. The real reason is money. Today's generation of voters doesn't like to spend money, not like their forebears did when they built interstate highways and rocket ships to the moon. Although much of the route is on public property through the Tillamook State Forest, there's still too much private property at either end to make purchasing the land viable in today's economic climate. Government today could, of course, "take" the land, but it would have to pay for that right. Today we don't really just take anyone's private property without compensation. The days of doing that ended generations ago when we vanquished the Indians.

Had there only been a gap through the Coast Range 150 years ago, you can bet there would be a road through it today to Tillamook, but now, well, it just all seems like too much trouble. Besides, even for today's engineers that gap would have to be flat and smooth like the Wapato Gap for a road to really make sense, as we're learning a couple of counties south of Gaston, down along Highway 20.

There is a passage through the Coast Range between Corvallis and Newport, and Highway 20 was built along that route back in the early 1940s by patching together other roads like the ones that wander up into the hills around Gaston. The only problem is that the passage from Newport to Corvallis is not really a gap, but more a series of low passes through the Coast Range, and it's not flat and straight enough to accommodate today's highway safety standards. Over the years too many cars, log trucks, and even an occasional gasoline tanker have missed curves along the route, sending their drivers to their deaths. So the current generation of engineers is wrestling with a plan to blast hills and reinforce slopes to allow for a much straighter, flatter, smoother highway. They even have the money to do it, but the road has never been completed. It's not really fair to blame today's engineers for all the problems the project has encountered, however, because the plan actually was born even before some of them were.

The problem is that even with all of our current technology and equipment, a natural gap through the hills still can be important. Unforeseen mudslides and avalanches and unstable rock formations have delayed the Highway 20 project by decades, so the trip through Eddyville is still not much better than it was in World War II. The founders of Eddyville just weren't lucky enough to have the natural advantage of a good old gap like the founders of Wapato had.

Although come to think of it, Eddyville still exists, unlike Wapato. Maybe it makes more sense to say they weren't as lucky as the founder of Gaston, who had a nice smooth gap conveniently located just a mile or two away, and the cunning and resources to exploit it.

Still Waiting for
Our Growth Spurt

Like the rest of the West, Oregon's population has
exploded since Joseph Gaston moved to the shores of
Wapato Lake and established his namesake village. In 1860,
52,465 people lived in the entire state. For a little
perspective, that's about 5,000 people fewer than fill Autzen
Stadium on any given Saturday for a University of Oregon
football game.

The population around Wapato Lake in 1860 was
about 70, which likely was a sharp decline from, say, 25
years earlier. Those 70 people represented the first wave of
white settlers, but their influx was not enough to replace the
approximately 90 percent of the indigenous population that
died from the flu and other diseases the settlers brought with
them from Europe.

In the decade that followed, Oregon witnessed a
veritable stampede of newcomers, including Old Joe Gaston
himself. For the next 20 years, the population of the town he
founded would boom along with the rest of the state,
swelling to more than 200 by the 1880s.

But by the mid-1890s Joe Gaston had lost his railroad
and had grown weary of trying to eke out a living from the
onion fields of Wapato Lake, so he skipped out of his sleepy
town and moved to Portland to try his hand at running a
factory instead of a farm. Forecasters for the state had a
much brighter view of the town's prospects than Gaston did;

they saw a population boom headed to Gaston, which was, they wrote in the New Year's Day 1896 edition of *The Oregonian*, "one of the newest but will be in the near future one of the most prosperous towns of the county." The reason for this anticipated boom? The rich farmland, "especially Wapato Lake," which, "when fully developed will be enormously productive."

Turns out Joe Gaston was right about near-term prospects for the town he founded. He left and bought factories to supply Portland's new Industrial Age economy and rode the wave of people moving into the urban area, which accounted for most of the state's increase in population from 413,000 in 1900 to 627,000 in 1910. Meanwhile, pesky old Wapato Lake resisted efforts to fully develop it, and Gaston's population stagnated along with the puddles in the lakebed.

The town's population was not formally counted until the 1920 Census, at which time it had swelled from the estimated 200 in 1880 to a whopping 221. The city then added a grand total of six more people by 1930. Gaston finally got its first taste of heavy industry when the Stimson Mill opened in 1933, and enjoyed its first population surge, if the 106 people added in the next decade counts as a surge. The only other major development since then was the construction of the Scoggins Dam, but the anticipated influx of people from that project never materialized. From 1970, when the plans were finalized, until 1975 when the reservoir was filled, Gaston added only 20 people. "People are not exactly knocking down the gates to get into Gaston," a story in the November 22, 1977, *Oregonian* noted.

That story chronicled the three new houses built in Gaston that year. "One replaced a dwelling that was torn down. One family that had been renting built a new home, and one family that had been living outside the city moved in."

By 2010, 637 people lived in Gaston, up from 221 in the first Census back in 1920. Compare that to a town down the river, Tualatin. Tualatin is situated close to three major freeways to whisk its residents to the metropolitan area's booming high-tech industry. Tualatin was incorporated the same year as Gaston and started with an almost identical population. In 2010, Tualatin was home to 26,054 of Oregon's 3,831,074 residents.

The reasons for the disparity are many, but the irony is clear. Gaston was well situated to benefit from the factors that built the old American West, natural resources and the railroad. It was not well situated for the Industrial Age, which pretty much bypassed the town altogether, along with the freeways that replaced the railroad as the preferred transportation of the *new* American West.

Ken Kesey, Bobby Kennedy, Felix and Birgetta

Bobby Kennedy, Ken Kesey, Bill Murray, William Burroughs ... when you're a photographer of Clyde Keller's stature, you meet such people and, of course, take their pictures.

The pictures Clyde Keller took of those folks have been displayed at the Smithsonian and many of the country's other top museums and galleries. Of course in fairness, Clyde Keller doesn't "take pictures" any more than Ken Kesey "jotted down stories" or Bobby Kennedy "read speeches."

Clyde Keller captures the essence of people. His photographs also capture the time in which they were taken, such as the haunting, intimate portraits of Bobby Kennedy that Clyde took just hours before the hope of a generation was gunned down by an assassin's bullet in California. In one of Clyde's "pictures" we see the senator walking barefoot with his wife Ethel in the waves of the Oregon Coast. Then we notice that they are walking in the last place the sun sets on what we commonly think of as the American West.

The death of one dream didn't stop Clyde Keller, however. After his friend Bobby Kennedy died he set out on other pursuits, including capturing Ken Kesey's Wild West adventures with new friends Bill Murray, William Burroughs and others. Many of the images Clyde captured are from Kesey's property near Eugene. He captures the Wild West spirit with all its unbridled hope, but also with all its gritty reality.

At Kesey's compound near Eugene, Keller finds William Burroughs, scion of a Midwest industrial fortune. Burroughs wanted to reach beyond his aristocratic roots and connect with what he hoped would be America's future. Burroughs' poetry and prose speak for themselves, but so do Clyde's images of the man, looking hopelessly out of place in the dusty fields, wearing black suits, dark ties and starched white shirts.

Comedian and actor Bill Murray is in those photos, too, live from New York City but juxtaposed in Oregon. He seemed to be as ready for hot afternoons in the Pacific Time Zone as he was for late Saturday nights in New York, but that judgment is left to the eye of the beholder, which is, after all, the way Clyde Keller likes it.

In short, Clyde Keller has captured the images of some amazing people. Just ask him. "I love that image of Felix," he'll tell you, or "I have other great shots of Birgetta." Clyde Keller has known, and photographed, some of the most fascinating and famous people of our time. Yet this acclaimed photographer can recount in exacting detail his interactions more than 30 years ago with such luminaries as Birgetta Nixon, Felix McCullough and other rugged and ragged characters of the Gaston area. Some of the poorest people he ever photographed left him with some of his richest memories.

Clyde donated his time and talent to create a 1978 calendar to benefit the Rural Awareness Project, which hoped to fight the persistent poverty that plagues many of those who call the Gaston area home. On the cover of the calendar is a picture of Felix McCullough, looking out at his farm. Keller's photograph offers a palpable clue that there's more to the story, and of course there is. The farm Felix is looking at soon would be buried after Scoggins Dam created Hagg Lake.

Birgetta was the resident gadfly and historian of Cherry Grove. Birgetta was, by most accounts, an eccentric woman who filled her house with discarded odds and ends, including all the fixtures from an abandoned post office. Birgetta had a hard edge and strove until her dying day to clear her father's name of a manslaughter conviction. She suffered the loss of a son in a military accident and witnessed her beloved hometown fall victim to crime and drug abuse. Yet when Clyde Keller was commissioned to create a 1978 calendar celebrating the characters who built this area, he found another side of Birgetta Nixon. What he found is captured in his iconic photo that he calls "Birgetta Nixon's Kittens," which you can see on Page 265. Clyde's photo captures a radiant Birgetta next to her beautiful granddaughter, both covered with little kittens clinging to their shoulders and sleeves. In the background is Birgetta's home, cluttered with the mementos of Gaston she collected and clung to in hopes of preserving the history of the area.

Unlike William Burroughs, none of the people in the calendar look at all out of place; in fact it's hard to imagine them looking comfortable in any place, or time, except for the ones they were in at the moment Clyde Keller snapped his shutter.

Felix and Birgetta are long gone now, replaced by a new generation of people much like them, people whose poverty is belied by the richness of the memories they have created for those lucky enough to know them. Many of Gaston's most-colorful residents will go to their graves without ever visiting the fancy museums and galleries in which Clyde Keller's photographs hang. For one year back in the 1970s they didn't have to, as the art world came to them. Every month a different work of art graced the walls of their own homes as pages on the calendar were turned.

And as for Birgetta and Felix and the others in the calendar, there's some consolation if they never saw the inside of a fine gallery. Their portraits did.

Really, What's In a Name Anyway?

Throughout the West, road signs stand as monuments to the tribes who once roamed the land or to the pioneers who supplanted them. The signs point to towns and rivers and valleys that bear the names of great people who might otherwise be forgotten.

Take, for example the signs marking the Tualatin River and the valley it formed, both named for the Atfalati, the branch of the Kalapuya indigenous people who lived on the banks of Wapato (or Wappatoo) Lake in what today is known as Gaston. Because the Atfalatis didn't have a written language white settlers could understand, the spelling of the tribe's name is subject to dispute. Early maps and journals spell it Fallatine, Fwalitz and other variations that probably tell us more about the nationality of the mapmaker than about the tribe's preference.

Atfalati remains the name most scholars seem to prefer, but not everyone cares what scholars think, and over the years the spelling morphed from Atfalati into Tualati or Twality. In 1955, when the doctors who bought Jones Hospital in Hillsboro wanted a new name for their facility they sought to honor the tribe, and they spelled the name Tuality.

The Tuality Healthcare system is one of only a few things that carries that spelling today, but had things worked out differently 100 years before the doctors settled on the moniker, the name might have graced road signs from Portland to the Coast and from north of the Columbia River down into what is now Yamhill County. That's because Twality, and later Tuality, was the name settlers gave to one of the first four districts in the original Oregon Territory.

But the second wave of white settlers fought their way out West through Indian territory in the Plains, and by the time they got to Tuality they had no intention of honoring any Native American, and they changed the name to Washington when the district became a county. So while the doctors really were reviving a very old name, their spelling was considered odd because by the 1950s all the road signs marking other remnants of the name, including the river, the valley, the highway and even the town, were spelled "Tualatin," a far cry indeed from Atfalati.

The variations of the tribe's name can be explained by the language barrier, but one might expect the white settlers to get the names of the English-speaking pioneers right. And, sure enough, the signs pointing to Patton Valley, Bates Road, Matteson Road, etc., correctly honor the families they are named for.

One of the most famous names in the Gaston area graces the name of a road, a dam and the entire valley in which they sit. The Scoggin family should be very proud, except that all the road signs spell the name "Scoggins." This was not just a casual misspelling, either. Over the years, many locals referred to the valley with the possessive "Scoggin's," There also are many references to "Patton's Valley," yet somehow that never stuck; Scoggin's Valley did, except that the apostrophe was dropped by highway

195

department officials and mapmakers who never knew the family.

Those who knew better clung stubbornly to Scoggin. For example, in her 1976 history of the area, Birgetta Nixon did not bow to convention, referring throughout to Scoggin Valley and Scoggin Junction. She did this despite the fact that just a couple years earlier the state bureaucrats who decide such things had settled on "Scoggins" as the official name for the valley, for the road that leads into the valley, and for the new dam that created Hagg Lake.

In fact, it was the naming of the dam that brought the spelling war to a head, as purists decided to take a stand at the hearings held to decide what to call this mammoth new man-made feature. They argued at those hearings and in letters to the editors of the local papers, but to no avail. "Scoggins" prevailed, and the name still graces countless road signs.

The purists did win one battle during the war of words that surrounded the naming of the dam and the lake. Many maps of the time listed the three creeks that combine to form Hagg Lake as the Scoggins, the Tanner and the Seine. Correcting the spelling of Scoggins was a lost cause, but they came away with one victory: the road signs over the crossing of that third creek now correctly honor one of the colorful pioneers of the valley, Thomas Sain.

Finding Sain Creek is easy. Just follow Highway 47, also known as the Tualatin Valley Highway, north from Gaston and over the Tualatin River until you see the road signs pointing to Scoggins Valley Park, just past the bridge that crosses Scoggins Creek. The signs point up Scoggins

Valley Road, which you follow past Scoggins Junction and then past the Scoggins Dam. You'll cross Tanner Creek and then Scoggins Creek again, and then you'll see the little road sign commemorating old Thomas Seine. Wait, I mean Sain. Thomas Sain. You know, that guy who lived here so long ago he actually knew the Atfalati people, before they even had a hospital named after them.

Why Onions Come
in White and Red

Stop by Kramer, Elk Cove, Plum Hill or any of Gaston's wineries and you'll overhear city slickers commenting on a wine's hidden flavors. "I taste plums," some might say, or "I detect just a hint of apricot, perhaps just the slightest whiff of tart cranberry ..."

But long before most of us ever even heard of pinot noir, folks in Gaston were producing wine that evoked other sensations. After swirling the wine on one's palate, comments might have included "Hmmm, the earthy taste of an early spring Russet potato ..." or "Raisins, definitely, and a twitter of citrus ..." and of course, "Ahhhh, the whispy aroma of onion ..."

Addie Fisher's recipe for Onion Wine includes all of those ingredients and can be found in Madelyn Heesacker's classic cookbook: *Onions Circle the Globe*, Gaston's most noted contribution to the culinary world. The recipes reflect both what was once Gaston's most famous product and the hearty tastes of the town's inhabitants. Hot Pepper-Onion Jelly and Apple-Onion Casserole are not for the faint of stomach.

Neither, for that matter, is Mrs. Fisher's Onion Wine recipe. Her directions include storing the wine for six months in an area "free from odors, such as tires or paint." The result, she assures us, is "a delicious cooking wine, but not intended for social imbibing ... although men have been caught sampling the product over the protests of an indignant cook ..."

The onions grown in Gaston were white and yellow, but the book also has recipes for the red onions grown hundreds of miles away in Eastern Oregon. In fact, the book has recipes from all over the world, all collected by the proud and prosperous onion farmers of Gaston.

The onions are gone now, and sadly Madelyn Heesacker's wonderful book is out of print. Today Gaston is known for its lofty chardonnays and pinots, grown high in the hills overlooking what once was Wapato Lake. The lowly onion and its enormous impact on the early economy of the area is largely forgotten and ignored, just like the lake in which the fragrant crop once flourished.

Still, tonight let's all raise a toast to Gaston's onion farmers ...

Right into the 'West Coast Danger Zone'

Most people wouldn't notice anything missing when they look at 1943 class pictures from the Gaston school district, at least until they look at the pictures from 1942.

Between 1942 and 1943 the face of Gaston changed dramatically as the town found itself at Ground Zero of the "West Coast Danger Zone," as Congress chose to dub the area.

The faces in 1943 class pictures are all white. The 1942 pictures, on the other hand, are full of smiling Japanese-Americans with names like Hashimoto, Yoshida, Mio, Nakamura and Furukawa. In some pictures, nearly half of the students are of Japanese descent.

Gaston's Japanese-Americans, including those who were native-born American citizens, were pulled from their homes in early 1942 and imprisoned in remote camps along the Oregon-Idaho border, suspected of being potential "enemy agents" and "saboteurs" by the American government and mocked in newspapers as "Japs" and "slant-eyes."

Hardly a word of dissent was raised at Congressional hearings in Portland to determine what to do with these scary "aliens." In the minds of the politicians the answer was clear: Seize their property and send them to internment camps. The answer was even more clear to the editors of Portland's reliably conservative newspaper, *The Oregonian*.

"As we see it," the editors wrote, "it is absolutely essential that the aliens be evacuated and that they be transferred inland beyond the Pacific Coast forest belt."

The children of Gaston, the ones with white faces who were allowed to stay, saw it all very differently. Clutching a prized 1942 class picture of herself almost 70 years later, Marge O'Rear points to and names each of her classmates who were yanked from school. As she speaks a smile comes to her face, but tears well in her eyes. "He was such a sweet boy," she says of one. "I knew her as long as I can remember," she says of another. "Oh, and she was always getting us in trouble," she says of yet another. "He was always a good athlete," and so on down the line.

She assumes the visage of the innocent child she was when this treasured picture was taken so long ago, back when she was Margie Cedergreen and the Mios and the Furukawas and all the others were her classmates. In fact they were more than classmates, she reminds her interviewer. Looking up from the picture, a tear now apparent in her eye, she shakes her head and says firmly, "They were my friends!"

Marion Matteson was 23 when Gaston's Japanese-Americans were swept away by the tide of fear, but he remembers them much as Marge does. In 1942 Matteson was a dairy farmer in Patton Valley; the Japanese tended to the onion fields in what once was Wapato Lake. Matteson lived on the land his family had owned since long before his birth; the Japanese were mostly renters of the "cottages" along Onion Lane. Yet he felt a kinship with his fellow farmers, and in his own way recalling their internment stirs

201

emotions similar to Marge's. Like her, he shakes his head at the memories. He wipes his face with his white handkerchief. "They were all just good people," 92-year-old Marion Matteson recalled in 2011, shaking his head again.

The onion fields are what made Gaston a center of Japanese-American culture. Most of the first-generation American-born *Nisei* worked the fields and rented single-story cottages on Onion Lane. Others, such as the Hashimotos, Yoshidas and Furukawas, were more prosperous and lived in "two-story houses further south," Marge recalls. The Furukawas were the most successful, parlaying onion-farming expertise and business acumen to become firmly entrenched as one of Gaston's most respected families in the 1930s.

By the time Pearl Harbor was attacked, many of Gaston's Japanese-Americans were *Sansei*, or second-generation American-born citizens, and some of them were among the first to enlist in the American war effort. The eldest son of the Hashimoto family was one of the first in line, Marge recalls, and went off to fight against the Japanese Army in the Far East. Unfortunately, this all-American young man had the constitution of someone raised in the moderate climate of Oregon, not in the jungles of the Far East, and he died in service to his country, succumbing to one of the tropical diseases that proved to be as deadly as the bullets of Japanese army rifles. Gaston's Peter and Jim Furukawa also were among the first patriots to enlist, and they were lucky enough to survive fighting for the country they loved.

But Gaston was more than just a center of Japanese culture. It also happened to be the center of "the Pacific Coast forest belt" that internment was meant to protect. While each of Gaston's Japanese-Americans had a distinct personality to those who knew them here, whether it was for being an expert farmer, prolific athlete, troublemaker or just good friend, to most Americans they all just looked the same. They looked like potential terrorists embedded near the cherished Stimson Mill and the forests that fed the war effort.

"*The Oregonian* editor," Ellen Eisenberg wrote in the *Oregon Historical Quarterly*, "argued that it was impossible to separate the loyal from the disloyal and therefore all Japanese-Americans had to be 'moved in the interest of national security.'" Soon Congress agreed and ordered the "evacuation" of anyone of Japanese descent, including almost a quarter of Gaston's population. Eisenberg notes the *Oregonian's* editorial board explored the treatment of Japanese-Americans and "compared it favorably to the treatment of 'civilian enemy nationals' by Nazi Germany."

As it turned out, only the much-larger city of Hillsboro contributed more citizens than Gaston did to the western Oregon "evacuee" processing center, and even then not by many. The center's personnel screened Gaston's *Nisei* and *Sansei* population for physical health issues, but made no effort to screen out the "disloyal" from the "loyal." In fact, by the time the processing plant opened the screeners were no longer allowed to even try to make such judgments. As reported in the May 21, 1942, edition of the *Washington County News-Times*:

"Pathetic cases were not missing in the wholesale shuffling of families. One boy, deferred from service until he had completed high school work, asked only to join his two brothers in the country's service, but had to be refused as the date for enlistment of Japanese had passed." Thus the young man was spared dying in a Far Eastern jungle but instead was sentenced to years of frigid winters and stifling summers behind the fences of an Eastern Oregon "camp."

The United States had adopted a policy of zero tolerance for anyone in the "Pacific Coast forest belt" unlucky enough to have a drop of Japanese ancestry. "Japanese ancestry means just that," the *News-Times* story continued, "and in one case affected a man and his children whose great-grandfather had been a Japanese."

The sudden disappearance of such a large portion of Gaston's population created a major problem for the town as its most-important crop, onions, awaited harvest in the silty muck of what once was Wapato Lake. "It is necessary that the farms be taken over immediately," the *Washington County News-Times* wrote in April 1942, before the Furukawas and others had even left their land. "because the ground is worked constantly almost from one crop to the next." The same article outlined the solution to the problem: the land had been given to "white farmers" to work, again before the Furukawas had even left for internment. The transfer of land was handled under the Wartime Farm Adjustment act, which classified the Furukawas as "Japanese farmers ... proposing to evacuate their land."

There's no record of any of Gaston's farmers actually voluntarily "proposing" to go to internment camps, but there are some records of what they thought when they got there. One such record is a letter one of Marge's friends, Kenneth Yoshida, sent to his Gaston pals. The *News-Times* summarizes his thoughts: "He writes they have games of all kinds, and everything is very agreeable except the food. Kenneth and his family have all become Americanized even in the cooking of food and Japanese dishes are not to his liking." The headline captured the scene quite eloquently: "Japanese Happy in Assembly Center; 'No Like' Jap Dishes." It's entirely possible that Kenneth didn't like the smell of his room at the assembly center, either; his temporary home was in the Portland stockyards, hurriedly cleared of cattle to house the Japanese-Americans.

Back home in Gaston, the tidy cottages along Onion Lane were quickly losing their charm. Famous for the colorful flowers when the Japanese-Americans occupied them, they now were nothing more than housing for migrant farmers. Within a couple of years, news reports about the houses no longer referred to them as cottages, but rather as "shacks" and "shanties." By the late 1940s, the once vibrant lane east of the rail line had definitely become the wrong side of the tracks.

As predicted, the "forest belt" around Gaston did become a target for the Japanese military, although the clumsy attacks – the only mainland attacks the Japanese made – fell far from their intended targets, hitting the beach or drifting far to the south, killing six people near Lakeview, Oregon, in May 1945. Ironically, Lakeview is not even part of the forest belt, but it is close to arid Tule Lake in California, site of the internment camp that was home to the greatest concentration of American citizens of Japanese descent on the West Coast.

The intended target for the Japanese in the spring of 1945 was the forest between Gaston and Tillamook, where the Japanese hoped to ignite another massive fire like the Tillamook Burn of 1933 and 1939, hoping to destroy timber needed for the war effort and to force the government to divert its wartime labor force to fighting forest fires. As it turns out, they needn't have bothered, because a couple months later the third catastrophic fire in the Tillamook Burn sequence broke out without the aid of Japanese bombs, blamed on the same thing as the first two: careless logging.

Until then, war-time logging had gone on mostly uninterrupted in the hills around Gaston. The timber industry didn't employ very many Japanese-Americans, relying mostly on immigrants of Scandinavian and German descent, who were never "evacuated" despite the fact that the U.S. was as busy fighting Germany as it was battling Japan. In yet another twist of irony to the saga of Japanese internment in the spring of 1945, while their families languished in internment camps in Oregon and California, soldiers from an all-Japanese-American regiment freed the survivors from the German concentration camp at Dachau.

While all this was going on, the Americans attacked the Japanese mainland with raids far more accurate than those the Japanese mounted on Oregon. With Nagasaki and Hiroshima reduced to piles of radioactive rubble, the Japanese monarchy surrendered. By the end of 1945, Gaston's Japanese-Americans were released from captivity, free to return to the onion fields of Wapato Lake.

The children were delighted when some of their friends did return, including the Furukawa family, which barely skipped a beat and quickly built their "Old River Onions" brand into one of the biggest on the West Coast. Marge O'Rear and Marion Matteson both recall that Gaston rallied around the Furukawas after their homecoming. "They were welcomed ... as part of the community," Marge says. "They were all likable and no different than anyone else."

The Japanese always had been welcome in Gaston, unlike the town's first wave of Asian inhabitants. Chinese immigrants were brought to town in the 1860s to help build the railroad that carried Gaston's onions to market. The Chinese workers toiled under almost slave-like conditions and with almost no sympathy from the white settlers. In 1872, a group of Gaston's railroad workers staged a brief uprising against their "boss." *The Oregonian* explains what happened next: "A boss workman at Gaston ordered some Chinese to go to work the other day, which they refused to do. He made some threats, whereupon the celestials rushed upon him with picks and shovels menacing his very life. He seized a pick handle and went for them, scattering them like sheep, and knocking some of them prone to the ground." At least there's no record of anything in Gaston like the hatred expressed toward the Chinese in other Oregon towns. Down the Oregon Coast in Marshfield, for example, residents who employed Chinese workers received anonymous letters threatening that their homes would be burned if they didn't send the Chinese out of town.

By 1945, Gaston had indeed become much more welcoming of its Asian population, but most of the once-vibrant Japanese community never did return. "It was hard because we were so attached to them," Marge says, the sadness still palpable 70 years later. The Furukawa family remained in Gaston for decades even as, one by one, the children moved away and the elders passed on.

Today Asian faces are nearly non-existent around Gaston. The Furukawa's onion barns still stand south of town, but the onion fields themselves are long gone, as is the railroad the Chinese built. The tidy cottages that became ramshackle shanties along Onion Lane are gone, too, replaced in part by the new fire station in the 1980s.

Not since 1942 have the class pictures of the Gaston schools ever again been filled with smiling, happy Japanese-American faces. Today, there are none.

A Conspiracy among the Conifers?

We all know that the great Tillamook Burn of 1933 was started by careless logging at a little father-and-son operation that chose to pull "one last log" after the industry giants had conscientiously stopped working to prevent wildfire in extreme conditions. We know this because it was the official finding of a commission established to find the cause of the fire and recommend changes to prevent future infernos.

So father and son Elmer and Bill Lyda took the fall for the fire and lost their logging company forever as a result. In some ways all the other little family-owned logging companies took the fall with them.

Until a few years before the 1933 fire, the area's logging industry consisted mostly of such small firms. The owners and their sons or brothers would line up small jobs and sell the timber they cut to small sawmills operated by other men and their sons or brothers. Before corporate giants such as Stimson took over the industry, Gaston, Cherry Grove and Laurelwood all were dotted with such sawmills; sleepy little Laurelwood alone was home to seven at one time.

The little mills are all gone, overwhelmed by the corporate giants. Back in 1933, the area's new corporate logging operations would have been happy to rid Gaston of its fiercely independent tree cutters as well, replacing them with corporate crews. But some of those stubborn families have persevered and still log the forest today.

The Tillamook Burn was a turning point in all this, and Elmer Lyda was one of dozens put out of business by the fire. It's not that there wasn't any logging left in the depleted forest, because there was plenty. There were so many damaged trees to be harvested that the commission members urged an immediate and massive salvage operation to harvest the burned trees before they rotted or were consumed by insects. The corporations sent hundreds of their own employees out to accomplish the herculean task of hauling these logs to the new corporate mill the Stimsons had just opened. No one had to pay reparations for the millions of dollars in damage because the Lydas didn't have deep pockets, and the wealthy timber barons who did were cleared of any wrongdoing. The commission had done its job, all wrapped up in a neat package.

For 42 years, the commission's findings went largely unchallenged. Elmer and Bill Lyda protested their innocence, but the fact that they freely admitted that a fire had indeed started in their camp that day undermined their credibility. The fact that they blamed the fire on unsubstantiated charges of sabotage by a competitor sounded like sour grapes. Surely, the commission's public record would stand ... if only there was a public record, which there wasn't.

The commission didn't have to meet in public, investigative reporter Ellis Lucia explains, because it wasn't a public commission at all, but rather a panel of representatives of the region's timber corporations, allowed to meet in secret. For his 1975 book, *The Big Woods*, Lucia tracked down witnesses to that day back in 1933 who told him that they had told the commission a story of the fire very different from the one told in the commission's final report. The story they told was of a fire much bigger than, and at least five miles away from, the one at the Lyda camp.

That other fire already was out of control and was in territory much more inaccessible than the Lyda fire, yet was never mentioned in the commission's report. The witnesses were credible, too, such as longtime Forest Grove Fire Chief Walter Vandervelden. Vandervelden confirmed to the *Washington County News-Times* that he had told both the commission and Lucia that on his way to fight the Lyda fire he saw a plume of smoke five miles away that dwarfed the one from the fire he was headed to fight. Among the many other witnesses who confirmed that account was eccentric Frank Watrous, who was in the forest that day searching for a lost Indian gold mine.

The origin of that fire never was determined. There was a Civilian Conservation Corps camp up that way, and there were reports of a wild party nearby the night before. Oh, and there were corporate logging crews working up there, too. But none of those people ever had to take any of the blame for the Tillamook Burn in the secret corporate commission's report. The blame fell entirely on Elmer and Bill Lyda.

The Lydas didn't have to bear the penalty alone, however. They ended up sharing that with dozens of other father and son operations in little towns like Gaston, families that never recovered from the Tillamook Burn, or from corporate control of the forests.

Lights On! Lights Out!

In about 1910, Cherry Grove became one of the first remote rural towns in the West to get electricity. Amazingly, 30 years later, it became one of the last remote rural towns in the West to get electricity.

The roaring headwaters of the Tualatin River were ideal for generating hydroelectricity, and the owners of two of the town's lumber mills were early innovators in rural power. Many years before most remote towns had power, Cherry Grove was enjoying electric street lamps, electric stoves, even an electric railway. The folks of Cherry Grove were living large by the standards of 1913 Oregon; even 20 years later, for example, the wealthy Miller family went without electricity when their Stimson Lumber Mill opened over the hill and across Scoggins Valley from Cherry Grove.

Not only that, but Cherry Grove residents even had telephones in 1913. There was no way to make a call to the outside world, but nonetheless Cherry Grove had phones. By January 1914, however, Cherry Grove streetlights went dark and phones went silent when the six-month-old Lovegren Dam burst. The Haines Dam continued to crank out limited power, but most of its electricity went up and over the hill and across Scoggins Valley toward Forest Grove.

Marion Matteson was one of the lucky ones, because his family's Scoggins Valley home was hooked into the Haines system when he was a small child in the early 1930s. "We were one of I think three homes that had Haines power," Matteson recalled in 2011, "We felt pretty special."

But then the Haines Dam failed, and Marion learned what it had felt like for the children of Cherry Grove 20 years earlier. He shrugs when remembering what it was like to lose modern conveniences. "I guess we just got used to doing without," he says.

Fortunately, Marion and his family didn't have to do without for too many years. With the modern, booming Stimson Mill as the valley's cornerstone, surrounding homes found themselves wired once more. Most people in Cherry Grove were not so lucky. By the 1930s, an entire generation had grown up without enjoying the electricity their parents had gotten a taste of so long before. Now, with the country stuck in the throes of its worst Depression ever, the prospect of getting electric lights didn't seem very bright in Cherry Grove.

Ironically, it would be the Great Depression that brought power back to Cherry Grove. By the time the Haines Dam failed, Franklin Roosevelt's Rural Electrification Administration was bringing power to places such as remote Appalachia and California. Cherry Grove found itself far down the priority list, however, and had to wait almost till the start of World War II before the Bonneville Dam was online and the wires stretched all the way to the roaring headwaters of the Tualatin River, making Cherry Grove one of the last towns to get electricity.

Business at City Hall is Strictly Personal

In small towns, personal and public business sometimes become so intertwined as to become almost indistinguishable. Gaston's City Hall is a testament to such governance.

Purists believe mixing personal interests and the public interest is a crime, but others might say that what goes on inside our City Hall is less of a crime than the pea green paint that covers the building's shabby exterior.

As in all towns large and small, people grumble about their taxes and waste in city government, but Gaston is, and always has been, a town of modest means. The City Hall is not a showpiece for the town, but then it never was meant to be. It was, after all, built to be a blacksmith shop, then the town's first automobile repair garage.

The blacksmith/mechanic who owned the business also was a volunteer firefighter and town's first fire chief, so when his department needed someplace to store its equipment, he offered up his personal space for the public good. Over the next century one thing led to another as personal interests and public needs evolved, and the building evolved with them, resulting in the humble City Hall you see today on Front Street.

If you look beneath the faded paint, you'll see that the building also is a monument to the American Dream, a testament to the aspirations of the immigrants who built the area, and to the resilient spirit of a proud community. But we're getting way ahead of ourselves.

The interior of the building is as rough around the edges as the exterior, but it's kept clean and neat by the town's only two employees, both long-time employees who take a deep personal interest in the lives of the public they serve. Almost every day residents drop by to pay a water bill or to conduct other business and end up staying to chat with Margaret, the town clerk, about the doings around town.

On one sunny Spring day, for example, the visitor was a stranger from out of town who had seen a bewildered old woman on the side of the highway and stopped to see if she needed help. The old woman told the kindly stranger that Margaret at City Hall would know how to help her, so the stranger gave her a lift to the drab little building.

Once inside, the lonely old woman asked Margaret what happened to the taxicab company down the street. It was such a lovely day she had decided to walk the few blocks down the hill from her home to do her shopping at "Ralph's Pretty Good Gaston Market," more commonly known as "the Market" and Gaston's other nexus of personal and public business. But after leaving the market, she realized that she had bought too many canned goods to make it back up the hill on foot, so instead she wandered down the sidewalk to the cab company, only to find it was no longer there, which caused the bewilderment the kindly stranger saw on her face and which led to this visit with Margaret.

There is no taxicab company in Gaston, and if there ever was it left many years ago, but this lonely old woman had no need to worry. She would get a ride home from

Margaret in a few minutes when Margaret took her lunch break. Margaret knows where she lives because this would not be the first time she had offered the kind old woman a ride in her personal car on her personal time, such as the day recently when Margaret made the 12-mile roundtrip to a bank in Forest Grove to help the old woman handle a financial emergency. Have a seat, Margaret told her, and we'll get you home in a few minutes.

Margaret then frantically searched the county's website for the numbers of social service agencies that could help her elderly friend, while the old woman sat in the cramped lobby and complained to another visitor about "the guv'ment" and her taxes. There was no hypocrisy in her complaints however; she was not asking for public assistance today, but rather for a personal favor from a friend who happens to work in a drab green building on Front Street.

That the drab green building is still there on Front Street is something of a miracle in itself. When the fire department's spanking new pumper caught fire that dreary day after Thanksgiving back in 1983, the ancient timbers easily could have ignited into an inferno. The shiny new pumper was a goner, but the building survived in remarkably good shape because of the quick action of Gaston's volunteer firefighters, who think of the fire station and its equipment almost as if it was their personal property. Men raced by car and by foot that Friday, pulling and pushing the pumper out into the street to save the building. As the pumper burned, they extinguished the flames inside the building and then saved what they could of the new pumper, which had been their pride and joy.

The loss was agonizing to the men of the department (no women would join for another decade). The town would be fine, because fire chiefs from surrounding towns were on the phone immediately offering Gaston's chief the use of spare apparatus and mutual aid until the pumper could be replaced. But that did little to dull the grief the men of Gaston Fire felt that day. The fire had been in the most public of all public buildings, City Hall. But to these firefighters, many from families that had staffed the station for generations, this building was a home away from home and the fire was a personal tragedy.

The fire in the station spurred the volunteers into action. Instead of dumping the burned-out shell of the pumper they chose to have an old friend, truck builder Gloyd Hall of nearby Cornelius, rebuild it. Hall did such a good job that the rebuilt pumper continued to answer calls for another 25 years, all the while proudly maintained as if it were the volunteers' personal vehicle. And within three years of the fire, Gaston got something it had never had in its 100 year history: Its first real dedicated fire station, across Front Street from City Hall and a block down Main Street at the corner of Onion Lane.

The fire station at City Hall had mostly just evolved over the years. As with so many other stories about Gaston, this one begins with old Joe Gaston himself. He came to town in the early 1870s, gave land to the town for a church and a school (although not a City Hall), then got bored with rural life and moved back to Portland in 1896 without ever bothering to incorporate the town that bears his name. In 1913, just weeks before Gaston died, a group of civic leaders got together to create a town charter. Their first order of business was to authorize a town jail, then a town fire department. The jail was built. The fire department was left to find its own home. There was no mention in those early notes of building a City Hall.

The next character in the story of how a drab old garage morphed into a fire station and then into City Hall is one of the civic leaders present in those 1913 meetings. Herman Krahmer wasn't born in Gaston, but rather on the other side of Iowa Hill, in the little farming community of Blooming. Many Gaston residents know Blooming today for little else than the 20 mile per hour speed zone past the Lutheran church and school on the otherwise 55 mile-per-hour Golf Course Road south of Cornelius.

But when Herman Krahmer was born, the Lutheran church was much more than an inconvenient speed zone. It was the center of a close-knit community unlike any other in the area. The church bound together a community linked by a common nationality and language, namely German. Herman's parents spoke only German in Oregon, as did he until he entered public school.

When Herman Krahmer visited Gaston as a young man, the town had two hotels. He chose the hotel where a young miss named Mabel worked behind the counter. Mabel was engaged at the time, but quickly fell for the strong, stern Herman. They married and settled in Gaston. Herman rode the train into Portland every day to learn blacksmithing, one of the day's steadiest professions. Herman was bright and good with his hands and became an expert blacksmith. He shod the town's horses, but also fell in love at first sight with the new-fangled automobile that was taking the country by storm.

A prosperous local farmer named Roy Bremmer had the first automobile in Gaston, but Herman Krahmer quickly followed, buying a used Buick. Many years later Mabel recalled the car, which she said had "all sorts of brass on it, and carbide lights …," but no doors, which was a major problem on Gaston's rutted and alternately dusty or muddy roads. Herman Krahmer was good at fixing problems, however, especially when they involved anything mechanical. He searched junkyards until he found doors for the old Buick and, for that matter, any other part the car needed.

Blacksmithing was a dead-end career for many when the automobile came along, but not for industrious folks such as Herman Krahmer. For Herman, working with metal just came naturally and he didn't care if the steel was attached to wagons, horses or cars. His shop evolved into a machine shop, and the town of Gaston embraced his new endeavor, just as it had Krahmer himself. In time Krahmer's business evolved into the Crescent Garage, which serviced all makes of automobiles as well as carriages and anything else that needed fixing.

Herman Krahmer built his business while raising a family and while serving as Gaston's first fire chief. Back in 1913, Krahmer was one of the civic leaders who drafted plans for the fledgling town. "Whereas," the penciled notes tell us, "an emergency existed and to protect the town from loss by fire," $497 was authorized for a "Double Thirty-five Gallon Chemical Engine ... at once." Then they authorized the formation of a fire company "to appoint some person or persons to take charge of the fire engine and look after its welfare." Herman's peers could think of no one better qualified than he to look after the engine's welfare, so they elected him fire chief. Thus began the history of a person or persons looking after the welfare of Gaston's fire apparatus.

Despite all of his other responsibilities, Krahmer's mechanic business grew until he built a large garage in a prime spot along Front Street, next to the Ace Tavern. From the street the building was rectangular with a pitched roof over the middle third. Under the pitched roof was a large garage door, flanked on either side by large windows. The location gave Krahmer prime visibility for his business and convenient access to the fire department's fire engine, which was kept in a garage behind the Ace Tavern next door.

This scenario worked for other volunteer firefighters as well. Many gathered nightly at the Ace, providing for a quick response to fire calls. The tavern was so strategically located, in fact, that one of the five telephones around town that rang when someone called the fire department was kept on the tavern's bar. When the bartender answered the phone he was supposed to run next door and sound the siren, but often he could rouse a crew from those in the bar.

The Crescent Garage's proximity to the fire barn behind the Ace paid other dividends. In 1941, the existing City Hall had to be torn down, leaving the City Council without a home. At the same time, the fire department was outgrowing the single-car garage behind the Ace Tavern.

The answer was next door at the Crescent garage/blacksmith shop built by Gaston's first fire chief, Herman Krahmer, and now owned by another longtime volunteer, Albert Porter. A deal was struck, the fire department had a big new home, an annex housed the City Council, and everyone was happy.

This is the kind of mingling of public and personal business that might raise eyebrows today, but there's no record of any protest at the time. It was a public transaction, of course, but also a deal among friends and neighbors.

The arrangement worked fine until the 1980s when the fire department moved over by Onion Lane and City Hall was left with a gaping hole to fill. A group of friends looked at the space and dreamed that someday the town could have its own library. Sadly, Gaston had no plans to build a library and didn't have the money to do so anyway.

Gaston needed money for a lot of things, but the stagnant national economy of the 1980s and a depressed timber industry left the town, the state and federal government all strapped for cash. About the same time the library folks were dreaming, a group of parents were trying to raise money for a real park in town, with ballfields, picnic tables, and a playground. They asked the city for money and were rebuffed. Same thing with the state and feds. The sports complex was just a field of dreams ... until Rick and Gail Lorenz, Bill and Madelyn Heesacker and others decided to just do it among friends with donated materials and volunteer labor. Today, Brown Park is a testament to a small town's volunteer spirit.

The same spirit stirred in the small group of avid readers. Before long, Helen Raines quietly donated her collection of books – and a check for $50,000 – and Gaston had its own library, filling the space that the volunteer firefighters had vacated. The space was filled with volunteers again, too, as the friends took turns acting as the librarian the town could never afford.

There never was a grand public plan for what had slowly become the municipal center, just years of talking and hard work by small groups of personal friends, the people who make pretty much everything happen in Gaston.

Give Up? Not in Coach K's Gym

In rural Oregon towns, high school sometimes seems like little more than a roadblock on the way to a job in the fields or forests. Knowing how to operate a chain saw or prime a pump can seem more important than knowing how to parse a sentence or figure a prime number.

But when the curriculum fails to hold a student's attention, it's often extracurricular activities that do the trick.

Sometimes it's music. For many years John Harris taught band at Gaston High School. Students followed the baton in Harris's hand in school and often after school as well, joining the volunteer fire department, where Harris volunteered for many years. When not fighting fires, Harris led the department's band, which performed in parades and community events throughout western Oregon. Many of Harris's protégés found their way on to college, while others devoted their lives to the fire service.

Other times the extracurricular guiding hand has a rougher touch, as in the case of the legendary Coach K. In fact "hand" might be too tame a word to describe Henry Kaulia's appendages, which some of his former students describe as "bear paws." One such description comes from one of Coach K's football players who felt his coach's wrath while at a basketball game, taunting the opposing team as it was being beaten by Coach K's Gaston Greyhound crew. During a timeout, Coach K's paw grabbed the footballer's

224

collar while he delivered a lesson in sportsmanship. "Not in my gym," he growled at the exuberant, taunting fan.

Kaulia was one of many Hawaiians who attend college at Pacific University, and immediately after graduating from the Forest Grove college he took a job as athletic director at Gaston High School. For the next 24 years, Coach K touched the lives of countless bored high schoolers. Over the years Coach K had more than his share of winners, but for the gentle Hawaiian winning was not everything; he always demanded sportsmanship and scholarship from the athletes he coached.

On April 11, 2006, Coach K was coming home after attending the annual luau at his alma mater, Pacific University. His car left the rural road and Henry Kaulia was dead at the age of 45. In his memory, nearly every student showed up at school the next Monday wearing a Hawaiian shirt. Years after his death, tough Gaston loggers, farmers, firefighters and others remember Coach K with terms like "he was my hero" and "I loved that guy." As they remember Henry Kaulia, some have smiles on their faces, while others have tears in their eyes.

But they all have diplomas on their walls.

Dropouts? Not in Coach K's gym.

A Lost Legacy Still Etched in Stone

Wapato Lake is what drew them here. It's what they loved.

We took it and drained its life, and with it theirs.

We kept on taking until there was nothing left, except their name. Then we took that, too.

Tualatin, Tuality. We took those names and put them on rivers and roads, hospitals and freeway exit signs and even on a suburban town full of cookie-cutter homes and strip malls.

We stripped them of their homes and hunting grounds, then combed the earth for artifacts and took those, too.

We have few of their stories left, because we rarely even took the time to listen. When we did we didn't understand their language. And that language is gone now, too.

All that's left are some pictures on a rock in Patton Valley, a ghostly reminder that this land once belonged to them, and that their legacy still is carved in stone.

Sadly, we're not entirely sure what that legacy is trying to tell us. These petroglyphs have been so long ignored and neglected, buried under years' worth of blackberry and poison oak vines, that their very existence became buried in doubt. The carvings are high above the floor of a valley with a name, Patton, that is about as white

226

as one can get. Although, in fairness, the valley is cut by the Tualatin River, which we graciously named in their honor. The river is still there, of course, though not exactly where and how we found it. We carved out a straight, deep channel and stole the river's wild spirit. We even moved it south a few hundred feet, in part to carve a railroad and then a highway and in part to control floods like the devastating torrents of 1972. But mostly we tamed and moved that wild river just because we could.

What they carved in those rocks high above the valley floor has lasted longer than the railroad did, and much longer than the mill the railroad was built to serve. What they carved in that valley lasted much longer than the dam we built to tame the Tualatin. That dam, the folly of a man named August Lovegren, lasted just a few short months before nature reclaimed its supremacy.

What they carved in that valley endures, although their drawings no longer belong to them. We took those, too. We gave those rocks and the petroglyphs on them to Matthew Patton as part of a generous donation land claim. Although we told Mr. Patton that the federal government was the one who donated that land, I think we all know who really gave it up. The Tualatins were the ones who "donated" the land when we broke the Treaty of 1851 and took their home. They had willingly given us their trust, but then we took that, too.

The rock those petroglyphs are on changed hands several times after Matthew Patton died. Some of the owners were proud of the carvings, while others cursed them because they feared the government would put restrictions on their land. Some even feared that those restrictions would amount to the "taking" of their land. But we know in this country that ownership of land is sacred and must not be taken from the people who live on it. At least we know that now.

So worried were some of Matthew Patton's successors that the exact location of those petroglyphs became lost over time to all but a few. Some longtime locals even swear the carvings are on the south side of the valley, but they're not. They're on the north side, guarded by barbed wire and "no trespassing" signs. They're also guarded by something even more powerful, however. The path to the petroglyphs is blocked by a fortress of blackberry brambles, which almost seem to be the revenge of those who carved the story in that rock, but they are not. In reality, the blackberries that ferociously guard the carvings were brought here from the Himalayas, another of *our* follies, not theirs. And as if the signs and fences and thickets of blackberries are not enough to keep the curious from the carvings, there's yet another weapon. Poison oak. Lots of it.

Poison oak was here when the people who made those carvings lived here, but they weren't much bothered by the horrible itching and wheezing that the stringy vines cause in us. Most experts say there's no scientific evidence that the Indians were naturally immune, however. More likely they were just much wiser about how to avoid and handle it. Perhaps not telling us their poison-oak secrets is their true revenge.

The petroglyphs are so heavily guarded that even some of the people who have owned the land never saw them. One such owner was an elderly lady who couldn't make the steep climb through the poison oak and brambles. Although she hadn't seen them, she cherished their presence, and she was thrilled when a researcher who specializes in petroglyphs asked her in the late 1960s if she could search for the carvings and document them in pictures. The researcher had taken pictures of dozens of other petroglyphs, but never of these elusive Gaston carvings.

So the researcher climbed the cliff and found the carvings. Soon afterward she sent the landowner a note of gratitude on a card she had made herself with a petroglyph picture on the front. The landowner cherished that picture, and when Birgetta Nixon wrote her history book about the Patton Valley, the photograph found a place of honor in its pages. Birgetta wrote a heartfelt tribute to the Indians, lamenting the fact that so little has been written of their history.

The picture in Birgetta Nixon's book is the only image of the petroglyphs many people in Gaston have, but it isn't an image researchers take seriously. It's not even close. The images researchers have clung to since the carvings were documented in 1889 by an anthropologist from Seattle are far less intricate than Birgetta's image. More primitive still are rubbings of a possibly different set of Patton Valley petroglyphs made later by another researcher.

Over the decades, researchers have speculated that perhaps there are two sets of carvings in Patton Valley. When Birgetta's book came out, they wondered if there might be three sets. Perhaps those who believe there are pictures on the valley's south wall are correct after all. The two more primitive sets are, after all, consistent with the style of Northwest tribes, although one of the sets is associated with tribes from the other side of the Coast Range mountains. The tribes in Patton Valley didn't like those folks and probably didn't invite them over to carve on rocks with them. Adding to the mystery, Birgetta's image looks as though it was carved by tribes who lived more than 100 miles away, across the treacherous passes of the Cascades and rapids of the Columbia.

All that confusion, coupled with the fact that the exact location of the carvings had become lost to history, eventually led some to believe the petroglyphs were myths or perhaps hoaxes carved by white people. The latter theory would be consistent with the rest of our behavior in the past 175 years or so. Maybe we stole their cherished art form and casually slapped it on a rock.

In this case, however, it appears the petroglyphs in Patton Valley are not ours, never were, and never really will be. Dogged research by amateur archaeologist Paul Lyons and others has proved the petroglyphs exist. In fact, I now have seen them for myself. Their research also supports the theory that the carvings are real and match the style of both the natives of the Patton Valley and those of the Pacific Coast, who most likely sneaked in and left them as an early form of graffiti. The petroglyphs are indeed just about the only thing we haven't taken or destroyed. They are not hoaxes, and they are not myths.

Well, except for that image in Birgetta Nixon's book. Really it's probably too harsh to label it with either pejorative label, however. Let's just call it a misunderstanding. Paul Lyons unraveled this mystery, too. Paul is a friend of Rachel Kester, the researcher who took the picture. Rachel did find the Patton Valley petroglyphs and took pictures of them, which she later made into cards. Therein lay the problem. Rachel made cards from pictures she took of all the petroglyphs she documented, not just the ones in Patton Valley, and the image on the gracious thank you card she sent to the landowner actually was of a carving near Arlington, Oregon, more than 100 miles away, across the treacherous passes of the Cascades and rapids of the Columbia. Rachel didn't intend to deceive. She just didn't know the landowner had never seen the carvings on her own property.

Birgetta had no intention of deceiving, either, but did what so many of us do when we attempt to relate the history of people we don't know: either create or perpetuate misinformation. I think Birgetta would agree that nothing we write about the indigenous people of our area is etched in stone.

So although not the ones in Birgetta's book, there are indeed petroglyphs in Patton Valley carved by Northwest tribes, including the Tuality people who so loved Wapato Lake and the hunting and fishing grounds of what we now call Patton Valley. Purists might call them the Atfalati people, or just apply the even broader designation of Kalapuya, which encompasses even more of the indigenous people we pushed off the land. We're not sure what to call them because we never really asked them, or at least rarely took the time to understand what they were trying to tell us. Whoever they were, we since have lumped them together with remnants of other tribes on the Grand Ronde reservation, which is, if nothing else, easier for us to spell.

Still, it's sad that we don't have more of their stories, but we were just too busy for small talk back in those days. We were busy draining their lakes and clearing their land.

We were busy replacing the villages they had lived in for centuries with dams and railroads and sawmills, most of which were gone within years or maybe a few decades, most victims of our folly.

However, we always replace fallen mills and dams and railroads with other lasting monuments to our Manifest Destiny, so our mark is here to stay, or so we think. Theirs is gone forever, stolen with broken treaties or crushed with bulldozers.

It's almost as if they never lived here, as if this land never meant as much to them as it does to us.

There's nothing left at all of their presence, except for their names on buildings and rivers and highways and towns, and a few crude drawings on a rock high above the Tualatin River in what is now called Patton Valley.

The drawings are about the only message they left for us in their own voice and of their own hand, and we don't even know what that message means.

Perhaps it's a warning to us from a people too wise to drain a lake, too simple to import invasive brambles from distant continents, and too tough to fall victim to the ravages of a puny little vine like poison oak.

A Creek With No Name

Swollen with the rains of winter, the creek crashes down the Chehalem Mountains and becomes a gathering place for deer and other wildlife. By the end of a hot, dry summer, however, it becomes an insignificant trickle.

The creek is so insignificant in the minds of most people that it doesn't even have a name. Yet to a select few, the creek has had an almost mystical draw, a draw that is at its strongest when the creek is at its lowest, most serene stage in the late Oregon summer, when even knowing it exists makes one feel as though he is privy to a secret.

In fact, the little creek holds many secrets and one must listen closely before those mysteries are revealed. Some surprises are pleasant, such as the little waterfalls along its descent. Others are haunting, such as a professor's unfulfilled dreams or the death of a bright young man. And then there's the mystery of the young woman in cut-off jeans. Hers was a mystery that made headlines nationally and yet wouldn't resolve itself for decades for the people who live along the creek with no name.

I was drawn to the creek in late summer, in September of a brutally hot year. I knew none of its secrets on that day when my wife and I decided on the spot to buy our little stretch of the creek. In fact, the creek itself was a secret on that day, so buried in blackberry brambles that we didn't even know it was there. "That's funny," I said as I read the property description, "This is supposed to be 'waterfront property.'" "It is," the Realtor replied, "there's a creek right over here." After about five minutes of searching in the thickets, we finally caught a glimpse of what we thought was water.

I didn't care about the creek. I just wanted a quiet retreat from a life lived in cities, chasing dreams that had long since run dry. Earlier that summer I had suddenly quit my 30-year career as a journalist, and we craved the anonymity this little valley offered. Although I had spent decades 30 miles away in Portland, I never even knew this little valley existed. I never knew about the large Seventh-day Adventist Academy at the base of the creek, or of the close-knit religious community of Laurelwood that had grown up around it.

None of our friends back in Portland knew about it, either, which is just the way most people in the valley wanted it. Privacy and serenity were what drew the Academy's founders to this spot exactly 100 years before we stumbled on the valley. As we slowly got to know our new neighbors I learned that they, too, cherished the almost mysterious quality of the place. The valley always has been a tranquil oasis, hidden from nearby Portland behind imposing Bald Peak, and cut off even from nearby Gaston, from which we get our mail, public schools and fire service, but little else.

The tranquility is what drew the college professor here many decades ago, and what drew the young woman in her cut-off jeans back in the hippie heyday of the 1970s. For the 100 years of the community's history almost nothing has ever disrupted the tranquility, except maybe for a single week that brought ferocious fires and a gruesome mass murder. That week was late in one of the most brutal summers in Oregon history; a summer so brutal the little creek with no name briefly disappeared.

The summer we moved in wasn't quite as hot, so the creek never completely dried up, a fact made obvious our first night in the house. As the sun went down, an enormous roar emerged from where the Realtor assured us the creek lay. Frogs – hundreds of them – began to croak as if on cue, growing so loud we couldn't sleep. Then just as suddenly they went silent ... only to erupt in song again a couple minutes later.

As much as I wanted to discover this mysterious little creek, the 12-foot-high blackberry brambles were daunting and the house needed my immediate attention, so we went the first winter without ever seeing it. The next spring, however, I set out to tame the jungle of thorns. I hacked a tunnel through the brush and finally got my first real look at the creek. What I saw made me sick to my stomach.

The creek had been used as a junkyard, clogged with construction debris, automobile parts, coils of rusted barbed wire, even discarded toys and clothing. I spent the next month clearing the bank on one side of the creek so I could collect all the debris and garbage. I hired a garbage hauler and we filled his truck with wet, muddy junk.

About this time one of our neighbors came over to thank me for restoring the creek. He told me that as a child he played along this stretch of water, which was then owned by a professor at a college a couple hundred miles away. The professor and his wife spent their summers here while dreaming of the day they could retire to a little home along this creek with no name that bisected their land. In the meantime they let the children swing from the large maples that lined the creek.

As we spoke, he pointed to one maple in particular, just on the other side of the creek, the side I had yet to clear. I thought he must have been daring as a child, because it looked as if the maple sat on a hill about 15 feet above the water, with the lowest limb another 15 feet up the massive trunk. I looked at the steep, blackberry-covered hill and dreaded having to scale it to clear the brush, but I decided that I better get started, and the next day I peeled off a layer of blackberry vines about two feet thick.

All I found was another layer of blackberries. I slashed at the brambles with a machete, expecting at any moment to hit dirt or rock. Instead I just kept slashing deeper into the thicket until I realized there was no hill. What I thought was a hill actually was just decades worth of blackberry vines that had grown up and over a large branch of the maple. The remains of a rope swing still hung from the branch. I stood in amazement, wondering how many years of neglect it must have taken to create this mess.

Most of the debris I had collected was of indeterminate age. Nothing looked to be of particularly recent vintage, but nothing looked like an antique, either. My first solid clues came in new trash at the base of what I had thought was the hill. The first was a faded, muddy, deflated basketball commemorating the Portland Trail Blazers' 1976 NBA championship. The next was a small bottle tucked in a pile of debris. It was a bottle of prescription medicine, with pills still inside, filled by a pharmacist in 1977. Taken together, these clues led me to believe that something must have happened in the late 1970s to bring a sudden stop to the days of neighborhood children playing in this spot.

My creek-restoration effort was noticed by a number of neighbors, some who had answers to some of my questions about the creek and others hoping I would have answers for them. One day as I mowed our half acre of grass with a push reel mower I noticed an old man at the fence, stooped over his walker as he watched me.

He told me how glad he was to see someone working on the land without power tools. He explained that he owned farmland down the valley but was staying with the people in the house next to ours while recovering from surgery. "That's why I have this," he said, gesturing his gnarled hand at the walker in front of him. "When you're 95 your bones don't heal like they used to." He apologized several times for bothering me, but it was clear he wanted to talk. He talked about the benefits of living in the close-knit religious community and having neighbors to care for him in his time of need, but quickly assured me that he would be back living independently very soon.

"Have you lived here all your life?" I asked him. "Oh, no," he said with another wave of his hand, "just since 1942." "1942!" I replied. "I bet you have seen a lot of changes in the valley." "No," he said after a pause. "Mostly just that everything needs a motor on it now. I don't even think people know what half these things do, but if it has a motor they need one." He said he never had used motorized implements on his land, and until today didn't think there was anyone left who felt like he did.

Then he waved his walker in the general direction of our stream. "And I like what you're doing with that crick," he said. "Water is life." I listened as he spoke disapprovingly about how over the years neighbors had sought to control the creeks in the valley, damming them, diverting them or burying them in culverts. I asked him if he would be willing to sit down some time and talk more about the history of the valley. "Oh, don't bother," he said. "No one wants to dig up the past. And no one wants to listen to an old man, so I'll let you get back to work." I thanked him for his time. As he turned to leave, I asked "Does this creek have a name?" He cocked his head and thought. "No, I don't think so," he replied. "Does it need one?"

Next it was time for me to play the part of oldtimer. As I worked one day several students from the missionary school that moved into the Academy buildings down the road approached me. Resigned to an evangelical spiel I smiled and welcomed them. They echoed the sentiments of the 95-year-old, telling me how amazed and pleased they were to see me working with my hands, without the aid of power tools. These students had come from places around the world to prepare for missions to other places around the world, and part of what they were learning was to help spread the word about organic and sustainable farming. One young man from Germany expressed sadness that his father and grandfather had been missionaries when they were young, and helped spread the word about fertilizers and pesticides; now he was being sent out into the world to help farmers unlearn what his forebears had taught them. He told me that another emphasis would be on encouraging villagers to protect and preserve creeks and waterways as sources of drinking water and irrigation. "People here don't appreciate how lucky they are to have all this water."

My cleanup efforts continued to attract attention. Soon after my encounter with the missionaries, the young man who had just bought the property the stream flows into as it leaves mine rode his four-wheel all-terrain vehicle the hundred feet or so from his house to where I was working. He introduced himself as "Josh," and he stood out from most the other neighbors. First, he was in his early 20s, a sharp contrast to the general range of 50 to 100 for the other neighbors I had met. Second, he lacked the quiet reserve of the church members in the valley, who were friendly when approached but shy and loathe to intrude into the business of others.

Josh was confident, outgoing and full of questions. "Do you know where the property markers are?" he asked. I showed him ours and he asked if I could help him locate the markers for the far side of his property, where the creek left to complete the rest of the short journey to its juncture with the much larger Hill Creek. I grabbed my metal detector and plat map and we spent the next couple hours searching for the buried metal pins. As we searched along the banks of the creek he laughed and admitted that he hadn't even realized the creek was there when he first saw the property on a late summer day. "What's its name?" he asked. "I've lived around here forever and never even knew it was here. I'm going to get out here and fix up my stretch."

Josh explained that he grew up just a couple of miles away but bought a big house about 15 miles away so he could be closer to his job in the county seat of Hillsboro. He and his young wife soon discovered the big house was a little too big for them to comfortably afford, so they had downsized into the house here next to the creek. With a baby on the way, they decided they needed to make every penny count until they could afford to move into a nicer house again. "It must have hurt to give up that big house," I told him. "Ah, we're not worried," he responded confidently. "We're young and we have our whole lives ahead of us." Sure enough, in less than a year they were gone, moving up to a better house.

I met the people who bought Josh's house soon afterward in a very unusual way. I met them at another neighbor's house ... a house that was now on fire. I saw the fire and raced to make sure no one was home. A man I didn't know arrived about the same time I did and soon we were joined by many other people from the valley, spraying the house with garden hoses and bailing water out of the little creek with no name to keep the fire at bay until the volunteer firefighters could arrive from Gaston, five miles away.

As the volunteer firefighters completed the job of extinguishing the fire, neighbors gathered on the hill at the base of our driveway to talk. Most of the neighbors knew each other and the owners of the burning house, because they all were members of the church next to the Academy. Others were not as well known, such as the man with the long gray ponytail who ran from nearly a half mile up the creek, through tall grass and blackberry brambles, to help save a stranger's home. As we all got to know each other, this gentleman with the ponytail explained that he had just bought his house up the hill after returning from years in Central America. Something about the little creek and the quiet valley just seemed right to him. He had been a champion hunter as a young man, but became vegan on moral grounds later in life. He felt a quiet kinship with the Adventists' vegetarian community, the same feeling my wife and I had felt a few years earlier.

The house fire along the creek stirred another feeling inside of me. I've never been a joiner, and I had cherished our secluded house because of the privacy it offers. Yet working side by side with this small community to save a neighbor's house, then watching as a bunch of volunteer firefighters risked their lives to complete the job, I began to yearn for a deeper connection. About two weeks after the fire, a newsletter from the fire district arrived in our mailbox. One of the items mentioned the need for help maintaining a website. I had been developing websites for almost 15 years at that point, so I volunteered to help. The department brass looked at my long career as a journalist and immediately began pressuring me to become the department's volunteer public information officer. I resisted because I knew very little about firefighting. Even more important, I knew nothing about the community, which I considered a prerequisite for the job. Gaston is a town where driving directions often take the form of "Go up to the old Jones place and turn right on the next little gravel road. Go slow 'cause the little Williams girl is deaf and won't get out of the road ..." I was still a transplanted city boy who didn't even know the names of most of our neighbors, or of the college professor who once owned our property and dreamed of retiring to our little creek.

Shoot, I didn't even know if the whole professor legend was true. Yet oddly, that's what persuaded me to become public information officer. I figured that I might be of value in Gaston precisely because I was not burdened by the rivalries, feuds, legends and myths that are common in small towns. So I joined and immersed myself in drills and classes and started responding to all types of calls, from raging house fires to the rescue of a horse trapped in Hill Creek, near where the creek with no name empties into it. My video of the horse rescue made it on to the national news and many others made the Portland television news. Soon I had gone from the consummate outsider to the person many Portland journalists turned to whenever anything happened in the area.

Take, for example, a tragic automobile accident in a neighboring fire district. A young man had witnessed the wreck, and stopped and carefully positioned his pickup truck to protect an injured motorist in the roadway. He went to the aid of the badly injured driver, armed with first-aid skills he had learned at his job with the county. Another motorist coming down the highway behind him, apparently distracted by the mangled cars, didn't see him, and the young hero died trying to help others. The poignant story captured the attention of the Portland media. Soon word spread that the young hero was from Gaston and my phone started ringing with reporters hoping I had known him so I could steer them to his friends and family for interviews. Some acknowledged that this was a longshot, but I was the only person they knew to call in the area. Others just assumed that I would know everyone in Gaston, even 31-year-olds with whom I had nothing in common. In fact, the next day I learned that I was just about the only person in town who didn't know the young hero, and I was reminded that I still knew almost nothing about the people who make this area so special.

But while my duties with Gaston Fire were broadening my horizons beyond our little piece of land, that land was becoming an increasingly important anchor for my life. I felt an almost mystical draw to this spot, a place that had utterly transformed my life. In a few short years I had gone from living in a highrise and wearing designer ties to taking care of chickens and the variety of crops that grew on the land. More than any other aspect of the land, the creek became a metaphor for my transformation. Taming the brambles and clearing the debris was one of my proudest accomplishments, although I wasn't sure why. I still routinely climb down to its banks to check on its welfare or simply to watch its waters trickle past. Sometimes I think about where that water is headed: First into Hill Creek, then into the Tualatin River, then through downtown Portland in the Willamette River, then up the Columbia River, where it hits the Pacific Ocean with a violence that makes the bar one of the most treacherous waterways on Earth.

Long ago there was another stop along its path, one that has come to fascinate me. A hundred years ago, Hill Creek emptied into Wapato Lake. By the 1930s, the people of Gaston had drained the lake to create agricultural land,

243

diverting Hill Creek directly into the Tualatin. In the county's official watershed records, however, our creek still is part of the Wapato Lake watershed, making this little body of water that holds so much importance for me nothing more than a creek with no name that flows into a lake that doesn't even exist anymore.

When I started writing this short story a couple of years ago, it was going to be about me, a creek with no name and a college professor who felt its magic just as I do. I intended to do more research on the professor, maybe even track down his descendants to learn more about what had drawn him to this place. Soon I decided to cast aside my journalistic instincts and accept the professor's story on its apocryphal merits alone. The story was just too perfect to risk spoiling with the facts.

The story was that professor had set his sights on the creek as a young man and nurtured the dream for decades; I had stumbled upon it almost by accident after we already had decided to buy the property. Still I felt a kinship with him because living here feels like a dream come true, the place I want to spend the rest of my life. Although we took very different paths to get here, our journeys brought us to the same place. I wonder sometimes if the kindly old professor ever let himself get lost in thought, imagining the creek's meanderings on its way to the Pacific. I bet he did.

While our journeys might well end in the same place, I hope it's under very different circumstances, because after all those years of dreaming of an idyllic retirement under the majestic maples, oaks and Douglas firs, the professor's story takes a nasty turn. It seems that almost as soon as he made the move to retirement he was diagnosed with cancer and was dead a few months later. It wasn't long after that the children stopped coming here to play and the creek fell into abuse and neglect.

So when I sat down to write this story it was to be partly truth and partly fiction. It was to be about how I am, in a sense, stealing the professor's dream that he never really got to enjoy. The creek was to be a metaphor about the restoration of that dream to its original splendor. I dreamed of restoring the creek to the way it was when the professor first laid eyes on it, or maybe even when the Indians first laid eyes on it.

The true stories of the 95-year-old man, the missionaries, the house fire, and the eager young neighbor all seemed to fit into that metaphor, each in its own way, so I decided to weave them in with the possibly fictional story of the professor. In the course of writing the story, however, I started to learn about people and events along the creek that didn't seem to fit my neat little narrative of life. Some of those things felt as though they might strengthen the born-again dream metaphor, such as the possible restoration of Wapato Lake. But most of the things I learned about didn't seem to fit at all, such as the biker gangs, the young hero who died on the highway, a couple of other fires and, perhaps most of all, the story of the woman in the cut-off jeans.

People in Gaston aren't always forthcoming about the area's occasionally unpleasant past. Some incidents devolve into secrets, sometimes whispered, sometimes forgotten. One of those secrets was whispered to me just as I was completing the original draft of this story. "Did you know about the murders?" a young man asked me one day. "They happened right by the creek."

No, I assured him, I had not heard of these murders. He explained that they happened long before he was born and he didn't know any of the details. I believed him, but I was confused. I had been public information officer for several years by this point and was writing a history of the department. Why, I wondered, had no one bothered to tell me about murders so close to my place? The reasons quickly became clear.

The neighbors I had asked about history over the years never mentioned the murders to me or, for that matter, to anyone else. It was a secret the close-knit church community had buried deeply immediately after it happened. The firefighters had never mentioned the murders either, although they were first on the scene. Firefighters love to tell stories of heroism and humor, but rarely dwell on heartbreak and horror, and this story was nothing if not heartbreaking. I went about researching the murders on my own, starting with figuring out when they happened. They happened, it turns out, in 1977, about the time the basketball and pill bottle were left on our property and about the time the creek became neglected.

They happened on a Sunday evening in August, at the start of one of the most blistering hot stretches in local history. But the story really began hundreds of miles south, and had nothing to do with Laurelwood or Gaston or the little creek with no name. Margo Compton (the name of the woman in the cut-off jeans) had worked in the sex industry

246

in San Francisco, specifically in a part of the sex industry allegedly run by a motorcycle gang. When Margo was arrested for prostitution, she agreed to testify against several members of the gang, and her testimony was terrifying. She said that gang members had held her tiny daughters, Sandra and Sylvia, hostage and forced her to engage in prostitution. Her testimony helped convict the suspects and police and prosecutors persuaded her that it was a good time to find some new scenery. She packed up her little twin daughters and sought out the most secluded place she could find, which happened to be along a little creek in a hidden valley, near a quiet religious school in Oregon.

By all accounts, Margo raised some eyebrows in the few months she lived in Laurelwood. Her attire and attitude were unlike those of the quiet people who had lived in the valley for decades. Still, she was friendly and her little girls were adorable, mingling with the other children on the church's playground and along the banks of the creek with no name.

By August 7, 1977, she had a new man in her life and things were looking good. In fact, on the morning of August 7, 1977, Margo's life story could have fit wonderfully into the narrative of this story. She had "retired" to the same creek the professor and I retired to. The true story of her life was even more unlike mine than the fictionalized version of the professor's, but it would have fit in fine.

But by the afternoon of August 7, 1977, everything had changed. Exactly what happened that day remained cloaked in mystery for nearly 20 years, but we know a few things about that lazy, sweltering Sunday afternoon. We know Margo had the front door of the house open and loud music poured out into the sweltering air. We know Sandra and Sylvia were seen about 4 o'clock playing in the cool shade of the creekbed, although the searing heat had evaporated most of the water. We know that the son of the new man in Margo's life was lying on the couch, on leave from the Coast Guard with his leg in a heavy cast from a motorcycle crash a few weeks earlier. We know that Margo had surrounded herself with two handguns and five long guns strategically placed around the small bungalow.

Margo had not told her new neighbors about her past. The biker gang had ordered its members to leave her alone and to not seek retribution, but still she was careful not to broadcast her whereabouts or her past. So when two men showed up that Sunday afternoon at a small store run by the church and politely asked if anyone knew where she lived, no one had any reason not to tell them.

A couple hours later, the volunteers of Gaston Fire were paged to an incident in Laurelwood and three of the most-seasoned members responded. All three are gentle, quiet men who selflessly devoted their lives to answering any emergency that might arise, but none was prepared for what they saw that day. Margo and the young man were lying dead in the living room. As soon as they realized there was nothing they could do, the volunteers left the house to preserve the crime scene for police. But when the neighbors asked about the adorable 6-year-old twins, two of the volunteers went back in to find them. They found them dead, shot execution style, in a back bedroom.

I was stunned to learn that Margo's story had transpired along this tranquil creek with no name, especially since it turns out I had known her story for years, long before I knew the creek even existed. I didn't move to Oregon until 1980, three years after the murders, so publicity about the unsolved crimes had all but dried up. But when two arrests and the resulting trial in the mid-1990s again brought the national news media descending on the state, I followed every detail of the horrific crime. Having studied criminal justice in college, I was fascinated by the fact that the biker gang was helping in the prosecution of their own members. The group's leaders had ordered members to not disturb Margo's quest for peace in the quiet valley, but what really created the unprecedented sight of members testifying against their brothers was the death of those two little girls. The hearts of even hardened gang members are stirred by images of innocent children playing on a swing over a little country creek. The feelings conjured by that image are nearly universal, but the name of the creek is of consequence to almost no one.

Likewise, when I was following the story in the 1990s as a journalist the feelings it evoked were not dependent on the name of the town in which the crimes occurred, especially since at the time of the trial I didn't know where Gaston was.

Now that I knew both the town and the creek, I still didn't know how, or if, the murders fit into my story of the creek with no name, which suddenly was taking on a life of its own. It gave me pause to think that here was another story of someone seeking dreams of serenity along my little

249

creek, only to see those dreams shattered. Good thing I don't believe in jinxes, I thought, or I might want to move. Little did I know I would find further evidence of a jinx a few months later while researching the fire department's history. As I catalogued major incidents, I discovered that four of the worst fires in the district's 100-year history happened within a week of Margo Compton's murder in August 1977, and two of them, both four-alarmers, were within a few hundred feet of where the murders took place. Rather than the idyllic retreat I wanted to portray in my story, for a few days in August this little creek must have seemed like it flowed from the gates of Hell itself. But the quiet residents along its path just locked away the memories and went on living in peace, not spreading stories of the past or intruding into the lives of others.

As a journalist, however, I do tell stories, and I set about rewriting this short story about my little creek, trying to figure out how to make sense of it all. Even as a journalist, however, I respect the privacy of my neighbors, such as my former neighbor Josh, the eager young man with his whole life ahead of him. I never even asked him his last name. Our conversations usually were about routine neighborly subjects and formalities seemed unnecessary, even when discussion occasionally veered into dreams and aspirations.

Or take the young man who died on the highway trying to save a strangers life. The story of how I chuckled when reporters assumed I knew him didn't seem so funny when, the next day, I found myself mourning with the young volunteers of Gaston Fire. It turns out they all knew him very well. I commiserated with them and helped set up for his memorial service, but never asked intrusive questions about him.

In light of the Margo Compton revelation I rewrote this story, this time omitting those two young men, of whom I knew so little. Josh still seemed to fit, but his role now paled compared to the professor, Margo Compton and, of course, me. The story of how reporters thought I knew the young hero seemed like a distraction now and besides, he was well-remembered with a large monument erected in his honor at the site of the wreck near Forest Grove, which I decided was a more fitting tribute to him than my silly anecdote. I rewrote the story without them and set it aside while I decided what to do with it.

As I waited to hear from publishers about the story I went on with my quiet retirement on the banks of the creek with no name. Along the way I learned that honoring the creek's past isn't always easy. It's not easy, for example, to keep the creek looking like it did when the Indians roamed the land when the invasive blackberries introduced by white settlers keep trying to bury it. I have broken several machetes in my probably hopeless attempt to stop the vines in their relentless effort to transform the landscape.

One rainy January day I grew discouraged in my efforts to be the creek's keeper and by the lack of interest from publishers in my short story. I came inside and logged on to Facebook, where I found my young volunteer firefighter friends commemorating the first anniversary of their friend's death on the highway near Forest Grove. Josh, they wrote, had died a hero, giving his life to help others.

Josh always had been like that, they wrote, helping anyone he could in his hometown of Gaston. Everyone in town knew Josh, they wrote. "Oh sure," I thought, "Everyone but me." As I looked at the picture one of my friends had posted of Josh with his young wife and child I was reminded again that I am an outsider in this town. Everyone else knew Josh and his beautiful wife and child. Everyone but me.

Then suddenly I was jolted by a memory of a day along the creek with no name, talking to my neighbor named Josh. Then I was jolted by a memory from exactly one year before this day spent reading Facebook tributes to this young hero named Josh. The face in the picture of young hero Josh was the face of my former neighbor Josh. The face of his young widow was the face of the young woman who smiled and waved as I drove past the house she shared with the Josh I knew. The child in the photo was not familiar, although I realized it was the baby born in the house next door, near where the creek leaves our property.

The young hero and my young neighbor shared a common first name, although I never had connected the two until this moment, staring at a picture of people I thought I didn't know. I had never pried into the lives of either neighbor Josh or hero Josh, but now I started asking questions. Of course that's the same Josh, the young volunteer firefighters told me; they just never saw the need to say anything about it. People in small towns often assume that everybody knows everybody else's business, and when it turns out that someone doesn't, well, then people in small towns can be very good at keeping it that way.

Exactly one year before that day, I had told reporters I didn't know the story of one of Gaston's best-known residents. I wasn't lying, either, because I truly didn't know him. I knew a nice young guy who happened to share a property line and a creek with me. I didn't, and still don't, know his real story, although almost everyone else in town seems to.

I do know his story is another tragedy, another dream crushed. Another story from this ridiculously short stretch of an inconsequential creek in a valley even few in Oregon have ever heard of. Another story that seemed somehow to fit into this strange narrative. A professor whose dream of life on the creek ended tragically almost before it was realized and a journalist unknowingly picking up the pieces of the professor's unrealized dream. An old man lamenting the loss of a lifestyle he loved and some college kids and an aging hippie intent on revitalizing that old man's way of life. A random house fire that changed my life in ways I never imagined and that led me to the story of a week of sheer horror in the sleepy community of Laurelwood. An optimistic young man with his whole life ahead of him and the heroic way his life ended much too soon. A bottle of medicine untouched for decades under the remnants of an old swing, both forgotten about the time two little girls and their mother, chasing the dream of a new life, died on the banks of a little creek in Oregon. It's a little creek with no name that flows into a lake that doesn't exist, but which might come back to life soon. If it does, it will be fed by a little creek loved once again by at least some of us who live along its path.

The story of the creek suggests many possible metaphors involving dreams realized and dreams dashed, the process of discovery yielding unexpected results, outside forces converging to shatter the innocence of a community, a past buried under years of neglect, and so on. But clumsy metaphors are nothing more than a way to try to make sense of a reality that is simply too complex to understand.

All of the events are, I'm sure, purely coincidental, tied together only by a little stream of water, a little thread of life, so utterly insignificant that no human has even given it a name.

Bibliography

Abbott, Carl. Portland, Gateway to the Northwest. Northridge, CA: Windsor Publications, Inc., 1985.

Abbott, Carl. Portland: Planning, Politics, and Growth in a Twentieth-Century City. Lincoln, NE: University of Nebraska Press, 1983.

Applegate, Shelton P. State of Oregon Department of Geology and Mineral Industries. "A Large Fossil Sand Shark of the Genus *Odontaspis* from Oregon." The Ore Bin. 30.2 (February 1968): 32-36.

Atkeson, Ray. Oregon, My Oregon. Portland, OR: Graphic Arts Center Publishing, 1998.

Azuma, Eiichiro. "A History of Oregon's *Issei* 1880 – 1952." Oregon Historical Quarterly 94.1 (Winter 1993 – 1994): 315-367.

Baun, Carolyn M. This Far-Off Sunset Land: a Pictorial History of Washington County, Oregon. Virginia Beach, VA: The Donning Company/Publishers, 1999.

Beckham, Stephen Dow. National Park Service. Cultural Resources of Patton Valley, South Fork of the Tualatin River Oregon. McMinnville, OR: n.p., 1975.

Beckham, Stephen Dow. Stimson Lumber. Portland, OR: ARCUS Publishing, 2009.

255

Beckham, Stephen Dow. The Indians of Western Oregon: This Land was Theirs. Coos Bay, OR: Arago Books, 1977.

Bergman, Brian. "Bison: Back from the Brink of Extinction." Macleans (February 16, 2004).

"Boos Quarry, Yamhill County." Oregon Bureau of Mines and Geology. The Mineral Resources of Oregon. 1.2 (February 1914): 29-31.

Brauner, David R., and William Robbins. The Archaeological Reconnaissance of the Proposed Lower Tualatin Sewer Project, Washington County, Oregon. Corvallis, OR: Oregon State University, 1976.

Carey, Charles H. A General History of Oregon. Vol. 2. Portland, OR: Metropolitan Press, 1936.

Cass, Penny L., and J. Ronald Miner. Oregon Water Resources Research Institute, Oregon State University. The Historical Tualatin River Basin. Eugene, OR: Water Resources Research Institute.

Cressman, Luther S. "Petroglyphs of Oregon." University of Oregon Monographs, Studies in Anthropology. Eugene, OR: University of Oregon, 1937.

Davis, Wilbur A. United States Department of Interior, National Park Service, and Oregon State University. Scoggin Creek Archaeology Final Report. Corvallis, OR: Oregon State University, 1969.

Decker, Doyle D., and Wilbur A. Davis. United States Department of Interior, National Park Service, and Oregon

State University. Survey of Impacts on Prehistoric Resources Tualatin Project, Second Phase. Corvallis, OR: Oregon State University, 1976.

Dobbs, Caroline C. Men of Champoeg: a Record of the Lives of the Pioneers who Founded the Oregon Government. Portland, OR: Metropolitan Press Publishers, 1932.

Eisenberg, Ellen. "'As Truly American as Your Son': Voicing Opposition to Internment in Three West Coast Cities." Oregon Historical Quarterly 104.4 (Winter 2003): 542-565.

Fagan, Kevin. "When Jailbirds Sing: It was the pure savagery of the four killings, which included the cold-blooded execution of 6-year-old twins, that led dozens of California's most notorious criminals to testify in a murder that had gone unsolved for 18 years." San Francisco Chronicle, Dec. 3, 1995.

Faubion, William. Treasures of Western Oregon. Medford, OR: Morgan & Chase Publishing, Inc., 2005.

Frachtenberg, Leo J., Albert S. Gatschet, and Melville Jacobs. Kalapuya Texts. Seattle, WA: University of Washington Publications in Anthropology, Vol. 11, 1945.

Friedman, Ralph. In Search of Western Oregon. Caldwell, ID: The Caxton Printers, Ltd., 1990.

Gaston Volunteer Fire Department 1955 Year Book and Directory. Gaston, OR: Gaston Volunteer Fire Department, 1955.

Gaston, Joseph. Portland, Oregon: Its History and Builders. 3 Vols. Chicago, IL: The S. J. Clarke Publishing Co., 1911.

Gaston, Joseph, and George H. Himes. The Centennial History of Oregon 1811 - 1912. 4 Vols. Chicago, IL: The S. J. Clarke Publishing Co., 1912.

Gaston, Joseph. "The Genesis of the Oregon Railway System." Oregon Historical Quarterly 7.2 (June 1906): 106-132.

Gaston, Joseph. "The Oregon Central Railroad." Oregon Historical Quarterly 3.4 (December 1902): 315-328.

Gatschet, Albert S. "Oregonian Folk-Lore." The Journal of American Folklore 4.13 (April – June 1891): 139 - 143.

Gatschet, Albert S. "The Kalapuya People." The Journal of American Folklore 12.44 (January – March 1899): 212 - 214.

Gatschet, Albert S. "Water-Monsters of American Aborigines." The Journal of American Folklore 12.47 (October – December 1899): 255 - 260.

Heesacker, Madelyn. Onions Circle the Globe. Forest Grove, OR: The Printery, 1984.

Highsmith, Richard M., and John L. Beh. "Tillamook Burn: the Regeneration of a Forest." The Scientific Monthly 75.3 (September 1952): 139-148.

Hill, Beth, and Ray Hill. Indian Petroglyphs of the Pacific Northwest. Seattle, WA: University of Washington Press, 1974.

History is Carved in Stone: a Tour of Pioneer and Tombstone Lore. Hillsboro, OR: Washington County Historical Society, 1987.

Hodge, Frederick Webb, ed. Handbook of American Indians North of Mexico. 2 vols. New York: Pageant Books, Inc., 1959.

Hult, Ruby El. Lost Mines and Treasures of the Pacific Northwest. Portland, OR: Binfords & Mort Publishers, 1957.

Hult, Ruby El. Treasure Hunting Northwest. Portland, OR: Binfords & Mort Publishers, 1971.

Ing, George. Wending the Way from Wapato Gap: Chronicles of Coping with Life, Strife...and Wife. Yakima, WA: Good Fruit Grower, 2004.

Jeffries, Jessie, Robert L. Benson, and Mrs. John Gates, ed. A Centennial History of Washington County Oregon. N.p.: Extension Study Groups of Washington County, n.d.

Jensen, Vernon H. Lumber and Labor. New York: Farrar & Rinehart, Inc., 1945.

Juntunen, Judy Rycraft, May D. Dasch, and Ann Bennett Rogers. The World of the Kalapuya: A Native People of Western Oregon. Philomath, OR: Benton County Historical Society and Museum, 2005.

Keller, Clyde. Pioneer Landmarks of Washington County, Oregon. Hillsboro, OR: Washington County Historical Society, 1978.

Kemp, J. Larry. Epitaph for the Giants: the Story of the Tillamook Burn. Portland, OR: The Touchstone Press, 1967.

Klooster, Karl T. Round the Roses: Portland Past Perspectives. Portland, OR: n.p., 1987.

Klooster, Karl T. Round the Roses II: More Portland Past Perspectives. Portland, OR: n.p., 1992.

Krahmer, Mabel. Interview with Elizabeth Buehler. Oregon Historical Society. 29 Dec. 1982.

Land of Tuality. Vol. 1. Hillsboro, OR: Washington County Historical Society, 1975.

Land of Tuality. Vol. 2. Hillsboro, OR: Washington County Historical Society, 1976.

Land of Tuality. Vol. 3. Hillsboro, OR: Washington County Historical Society, 1978.

Linenberger, Toni Rae. United States. Bureau of Reclamation History Program. The Tualatin Project. Denver, CO: Research on Historic Reclamation Projects, 2000.

Lloyd, Francis E. "Petroglyphs in Patton's Valley." The Oregon Naturalist 3.6 (June 1896): 84 – 85.

Lucia, Ellis. The Big Woods: Logging and Lumbering, From Bull Teams to Helicopters, in the Pacific Northwest. Garden City, NY: Doubleday, 1975.

Lucia, Ellis. The Saga of Ben Holladay: Giant of the Old West. New York: Hastings House Publishers, 1959.

Mackey, Harold. The Kalapuyans: a Sourcebook on the Indians of the Willamette Valley. Salem, OR: Mission Hill Museum Association, 1974.

Mallery, Garrick, and James Gilchrist Swan. United States. "Pictographs of the North American Indians, A Preliminary

Paper: Rock Carvings in Oregon and in Washington." Fourth Annual Report of the U.S. Bureau of Ethnology to the Secretary of the Smithsonian Institution 1882 - 1883. Washington DC: U.S. Government Printing Office (1886): 25-26.

Mallery, Garrick. United States. "Picture-Writing of the American Indians: Oregon." Tenth Annual Report of the U.S. Bureau of Ethnology to the Secretary of the Smithsonian Institution 1888 - 1889. Washington DC: U.S. Government Printing Office (1893): 104-105.

"Matching Stone Found for Pacific's Marsh Hall Rebuilding." Nov. 4, 1975. Pacific University.

Miranda, Gary, and Rick Read. Splendid Audacity: the Story of Pacific University. Seattle, WA: Documentary Book Publishers, 2000.

Mooberry, Lester C. The Gray Nineties. Portland, OR: Binfords & Mort Publishers, 1957.

Murrell, Gary. "Hunting Reds in Oregon, 1935-1939." Oregon Historical Quarterly 100.4 (Winter 1999): 374-401.

Murrell, Gary. Iron Pants: Oregon's Anti-New Deal Governor, Charles Henry Martin. Pullman, WA: Washington State University Press, 2000.

Nixon, Birgetta, and Mabel Tupper. Cherry Grove: a History from 1852 to the Present. N.p.: n.p., 1977.

Norris, William G. United States. Department of Agriculture. The Details of the Tillamook Fire from its Origin to the

Salvage of the Killed Timber. Portland, OR: Forest Service.
1935.

Old Yamhill: the Early History of its Towns and Cities.
Lafayette, OR: Yamhill County Historical Society, 1976.

"Petroglyphs in Oregon." The Oregon Naturalist 3.4 (April
1896): 56 – 57.

Pintarich, Dick, ed. Great and Minor Moments in Oregon
History. Portland, OR: New Oregon Publishers, Inc., 2003.

Robbins, Williams G. "The Good Fight: Forest Fire
Protection." Oregon Historical Quarterly 102.3 (Fall 2001):
270-289.

Roe, Robert B. "Notes for a Gaston Fire Department History
Report." Gaston High School English Class, 1954.

Roe, Thomas R. A Short History of Gaston, Oregon. Gaston
Community Library.

Ross, John R., and Margaret Byrd Adams. The Builder's Spirit:
the History of the Stimson Lumber Company. Portland, OR:
John Ross and Associates, 1983.

Schuck, Walter. "Gaston Petroglyphs."Oregon Archaeological
Society Screenings 6.8 (August 1957).

Seaburg, William R., ed., and Pamela T. Amoss, ed. Badger
and Coyote were Neighbors: Melville Jacobs on Northwest
Indian Myths and Tales. Corvallis, OR: Oregon State
University Press, 2000.

Snell, Earl, comp. The Oregon Blue Book 1935 – 1936. Salem, OR: State Printing Department, 1935.

Snyder, Eugene E. Early Portland: Stump-Town Triumphant. Portland, OR: Binfords & Mort Publishers, 1970.

Stearns, Marjorie R. "The Settlement of the Japanese in Oregon." Oregon Historical Quarterly 39.3 (September 1938): 262-269.

Steere, Margaret L. State of Oregon Department of Geology and Mineral Industries. "Fossil Localities of the Sunset Highway Area, Oregon." The Ore Bin. 19.5 (May 1957): 37-46.

Thomas, Lowell. The Wreck of the Dumaru. New York: P. F. Collier & Son Corporation, 1930.

Washington County Wanderings. Hillsboro, OR: Hillsboro Junior Women's Club, 1970.

Welton, Bruce J. State of Oregon Department of Geology and Mineral Industries. "Fossil Sharks in Oregon." The Ore Bin. 34.10 (October 1972): 161-166.

Workers of the Writers' Program of the Work Projects Administration in the State of Oregon, comps. Oregon: End of the Trail, American Guide Series. Portland, OR: Binfords & Mort Publishers, 1940.

Personal Interviews and Individual Resources:

Bell, Margaret
Hoodenpyl, Ronald S.
Lyons, Paul
Matteson, Marion. Personal interview. 7 Sept. 2011.
O'Rear, Marge. Personal interview. 13 Sept. 2011.
Roe, Robert B.

Libraries:

Forest Grove City Library
Gaston Community Library
Oregon Historical Society Research Library
Pacific University Library
Washington County Museum Research Library

Archives:

Ancestry.com
Forest Grove Independent
Forest Grove News Times
Gaston Herald
Hillsboro Argus
Oregon Journal
The Oregonian
San Francisco Chronicle
Seattle Star
Beaverton Valley Times
Washington County Hatchet
Washington County News Times

"Birgetta Nixon's Kittens," by Clyde Keller
Used by permission. www.clydekeller.com

Among friends

I never met Birgetta "Birdy" Nixon, although I feel as though I know her. Her crude yet beautiful book about Cherry Grove is what led Kris and me to write this book.

I never knew George Ing, either, but he also wrote a book about Gaston that got us started down our path.

Luckily, I do know many of the incredible people who help keep alive the history of this often-forgotten corner of America.

Some I already count as friends, such as Ron Hoodenpyl, who devoted 50 years of his life to the Gaston Rural Fire District, mostly as a volunteer. Of course there are all the other Hoodenpyls who helped with stories for both this book and for one I'm writing about the fire district. There's Jerry, Chip, Randy, Deon and James, among others, as well as Chief Roger Mesenbrink who was, after all, the first person to tell me about Birgetta Nixon's book. Then there's Seth Hedin, who is related to nearly everyone.

Others I met while writing the book, including Clyde Keller. Clyde's photos of Bobby Kennedy and Ken Kesey inspired me long before I ever heard of Gaston, Oregon. What a pleasant surprise it was, then, when we learned he also had captured the heart of this area in some of his lesser-known, but equally poignant, work. His gift of one of the few remaining copies of a calendar he produced as a fundraiser for the people of this area was an even bigger surprise, as well as an honor.

Then there's Paul Lyons. Paul is an amateur archaeologist who, by coincidence, was hot on the trail of the lost Patton Valley petroglyphs at the same time Kris and I were searching in vain. When I called him, he was at first suspicious, but soon generously shared everything he knew about these treasures.

And there's Margaret Bell. Margaret works for the city of Gaston. Her title is ambiguous, because it depends on what your issue is at any moment. Truth is that Margaret just does whatever needs to be done to keep the town running. Margaret loves Gaston and helped me immeasurably, even while juggling other tasks such as helping an old lady find her way up the hill with her groceries, which doesn't fit neatly into any of her job titles.

It's presumptuous to call some of the people we've met "friends," although Kris and I hope they might accept that title. Bob Roe helped me on another project, the history of Gaston Fire, and the records his parents left to the Gaston Community Library were helpful for this book. Marion Matteson prefaced his stories with disclaimers such as "I'm 92 ... I don't remember much," but of course he did and his humor and insights proved invaluable. Folks I met in passing, such as Ed Noyes, offered helpful stories as well.

Marge O'Rear definitely feels like a friend, after entertaining us with her stories and insights into the tragedy of Japanese internment.

Last, and certainly not least, is another man I never met, Ellis Lucia. You'll find Ellis' name mentioned frequently in this book, but not nearly as often as he deserves. I quote from books he wrote, but also from an amazing array of stories he wrote for the *Washington County News-Times* and *The Oregonian*. "I don't pretend to be God's gift to the Northwest literary world," Lucia once was quoted as saying, "But I hope a few of the books I've done will be remembered and kept as Western or Pacific Northwestern Americana. I like feeling that somewhere our national history is enriched."

Like me and Old Joe Gaston, Ellis was a newspaperman and, like me and Old Joe Gaston, Ellis Lucia turned to writing history later in life.

Index

About the authors

Ken and Kris Bilderback moved to the Laurelwood area of Gaston in 2004, mere days before the Seventh-day Adventists celebrated the centennial of their arrival in the area.

Ken grew up near Detroit, Michigan, and graduated from the University of Dayton. He spent 30 years as a journalist at newspapers across the country. His novel, "Wheels on the Bus," chronicles the wild cross-country trips that eventually landed him in Oregon, which has been his home since 1980. Ken also served several stints at the Freedom Forum Media Studies Center at Columbia University and the University of California.

Kris graduated from the University of Washington and spent her career in administration at the UW, Bastyr University and at Pacific University. She spent countless hours researching newspaper and library archives in search of stories for this book.

The authors' move to Laurelwood in the middle of the community's centennial was purely coincidental, as is this book's proximity to the city of Gaston's centennial in 2014. Yet another local centennial is on the horizon as well: 2013 marks 100 years of service by the Gaston Volunteer Fire Department. Ken is writing a book about that centennial as a fundraiser for the department.

Learn more about Gaston:
www.gastonoregon.com

More books by the author:
www.kenbilderback.com

Made in the USA
Charleston, SC
05 August 2012